APPLICATION DEVELOPMENT WITH POWERBUILDER

Train with Ravi

BY RAVI KUMAR PARAMKUSAM

Made with ❤ on the Notion Press Platform

www.notionpress.com

Contents

Foreword

This book on software development is meant for beginners, who want to learn software coding on PowerBuilder. There are techniques to develop screens, with the detailed use of the screens and their place in the software. If anyone is interested in having the source code they may contact these email IDs: ravi_kp_com@yahoo.com or ravikiransofttech@gmail.com

My Books website: http://ravikirantechnosoft.in /

Or https://ravikumar.azurewebsites.net

All my book links are available on the website.

Also, free pdf copies are available.

You are welcome to contact me for any kind of support.

Write to me @ ravi_kp_com@yahoo.com for a quicker reply.

Ravi Kumar Paramkusam

Software Professional and Writer

Date 13th Jan 2024

Preface

In my 30+ years of experience I have Developed many software for many companies in different technologies and different domains. I have worked extensively with PowerBuilder and Visual Studio developing Applications and web applications. This book is about how to start with PowerBuilder Software and how to program applications. It is assumed that you have some basic knowledge of using PowerBuilder. The First part is developing master windows for use in the development with inheritance and datawindows, the two pillars of the PowerBuilder for Rapid Application Development(RAD) tool.

The Second Part is actual development using these master windows.

Ravi Kumar Paramkusam

Date 13th Jan 2024

Acknowledgements

This is to acknowledge the developers who have worked with me all these years.

This book is dedicated to all the companies and developers, I worked for and developed software.

PART 1
Developing Master Windows

Chapter 1

Introduction

PowerBuilder is a GUI-based software development tool that follows all OOPS concepts.

Inheritance is the main concept in developing in 'PB' in short it is called, which reduces the development time.

PB is an evolving software. From v5 in 1998 now after releasing v12.5, they started naming versions by the year. The latest version is the 2022R3 customer release Beta.

Some say "Thousands of PowerBuilder applications still run today. Even though the platform is supposedly supported, its development has been slow in the past decade. It has changed hands multiple times which has caused the technology to become less desirable and lacking basic functionality from more modern platforms."

But it is not true that it lacks basic functionality, it is a robust program and 'datawindows' is the best functionality that exists on any platform. Datawindows allows to retrieve the data from tables and allows it to update the tables with just one command. It can recognise whether the data is newly updated, modified, or deleted and act accordingly.

PowerBuilder is compatible with all the modern databases. It comes preloaded with most of the database drivers. Others can be downloaded from their respective websites.

It has the latest functionality to update with JSON, XML, or any other type of data like Excel, CSV or any other table-based data.

New releases of the PB mostly focus on .net compatibility. From Version 11 conversion to .net, they started. The code can be converted to Asp.Net and ported to IIS and run as a web-based application.

The latest version contains Powerscript migrator, which converts PowerBuilder code to C# code.

Powerserver helps to distribute the PowerBuilder application through the web to multiple locations.

But first I will show how to create master windows for the best performance. This is the first step in developing applications at a rapid speed.

There are two main master windows one with a single datawindow for master data entry and two datawindows for master, details type data entry. Then there are two types of report masters. The first type does not use any retrieval arguments and is mainly useful for displaying master data and simple reports. The second report master window uses retrieval arguments like dates and other data. Based on the data selected the report is retrieved and there are buttons for zooming the data and sending it to a printer.

Development of Master windows

This is the single datawindow master window. The white space in the middle of the window is the one where we will place datawindow. I will show how the datawindow is made later in the chapter.

Now let us see what the page consists of. The ribbon containing the commands Save, Modify, View, Delete and Cancel is called a user object. A user object can be created and this object is created by placing buttons and writing code for the buttons.

Global variables

string coname, addok, am, fayear, module, machine, loc, usrname

string voutype, ind_pol, corp_pol, pre_auth, claim_reg, companyname, company, branch, ls_string, gs_fayear, gs_custcd, claim_proc, claim_set, mis_rep , ttype

date std_date,today

datetime lst_date,fafrdt,fatodt,sysdatetime

int level

long ctr,ref_no

char login,item_flag

int ts

DataWindow gdw1,gdw2

string gs_which_window

char o_flag, sales, stores,purchase, finance, setup, other

datawindow dw_x

datawindowchild dwc

string pay,fin,pname,g_logincd,g_login,stype

string chk, subaccd

real amt

long vouno

```
string ptype,ins_co,ins_type,contype
```

Instance variables for user object
```
datawindow dw_1
boolean commit_flag,save_flag
```
function: uof_reg returns none, input datawindow
dw_1a
```
dw_1=dw_1a
```
Code for save button:
```
dw_1.setredraw(false)
integer rtn
if delete_flag = true then
if messagebox("CONFIRM DELETE", "Are you sure you
want to delete this record?",Question!,YesNo!,2) = 1
then
        rtn = dw_1.deleterow(0)
        if rtn = 1 then
        parent.triggerevent("delete_event")
        rtn = dw_1.update()
        if rtn = 1 then
                commit using sqlca;
w_mastermenu.sle_1.text = "Record has been deleted."
                delete_flag = false
                pb_cancel.triggerevent("clicked")
        else
messagebox("Deletion Error","Related Data Exists
        pb_cancel.triggerevent("clicked")
end if
end if
        end if
else
        parent.triggerevent("save_before_event")
        if update_flag = true then
                rtn = dw_1.update()
                if rtn = 1 then
```

```
                    parent.triggerevent("save_event")
                        if commit_flag = true then
                        commit using sqlca;
w_mastermenu.sle_1.text  =  "Records  have  been
saved."
            update_flag = false


            pb_cancel.triggerevent("clicked")
                        else
                        rollback using sqlca;
                        end if
                else
messagebox("Save Error","Save has been cancelled")
        rollback using sqlca;
        end if
        else
                rollback using sqlca;
        end if
end if
dw_1.setredraw(true)
```

code for modify button:
```
dw_1.setredraw(false)
delete_flag = false
parent.triggerevent("modify_before_event")
if ts=1 then
        return 1
end if
dw_1.reset()
dw_1.insertrow(0)
dw_1.setfocus()
parent.triggerevent("modify_event")
dw_1.setredraw(true)
```
code for view button:
```
dw_1.setredraw(false)
delete_flag = false
parent.triggerevent("view_before_event")
```

```
if ts=1 then
        return 1
end if
dw_1.reset()
dw_1.insertrow(0)
dw_1.setfocus()
parent.triggerevent("view_event")
dw_1.setredraw(true)
```

code for delete button:
```
dw_1.setredraw(false)
parent.triggerevent("delete_before_event")

if ts=1 then
        return 1
end if
dw_1.reset()
dw_1.insertrow(0)
dw_1.setfocus()
dw_1.setredraw(true)
```

Code for cancel button:
```
parent.triggerevent("cancel_event")
```

Code for exit button:
```
if dw_1.modifiedcount() + dw_1.deletedcount() > 0 then
        if messagebox("UNSAVED CHANGES!","Do you
wish to exit without saving ?",Question!,YesNo!,2) = 1
then
                close(parent)
        end if
else
        close(parent)
end if
```

Next *code for the master window:*
Code for open event of the window:
```
dw_1.settransobject(sqlca)
w_mastermenu.pb_1.enabled = false
```

```
uo_2.uf_register(dw_1)
setbuttons(true)
uo_2.pb_new.triggerevent(clicked!)
i_height = this.height
i_width = this.width
sle_1.taborder = 0
dw_1.modify("datawindow.color='"+string(rgb(216,228,
248))+"'")
rr_1.fillcolor=rgb(216,228,248)
return 0
```

Code for close event:
```
w_mastermenu.pb_1.enabled = true
// the main window will open
commit using sqlca;
// all the pending data updates will be committed
```

clicked event of the window – useful for web application
```
#IF Defined PBDOTNET THEN
   dw_1.JavaScriptFile = "MyScriptFile.js"
   dw_1.OnClientClicked = "MyDWClickedEventHandler"
#END IF
****
```

Instance variables
```
integer i_height, dw_height,dw_width
integer i_width,error_flag
string i_dml_flag,colname
long l_rows
int finyear
```

Function setbuttons: Boolean a_type as input returns none
```
//this function sets the buttons as per the user type and
module can be reconfigured
//string add,del ,mod
//Instant   variables   datawindow   dw_1,   boolean
update_flag, //delete_flag, newflag,commit_flag
```

```
add='N'
del='N'
mod='N'
addok='N'
if level=0 or level>3 then
        addok='Y'
        add='Y'
        mod='Y'
        del='Y'
end if
if add = 'Y' then
        addok='Y'
else
        addok='N'
end if
if add="Y" then
        uo_2.pb_new.enabled=true
else
        uo_2.pb_new.enabled=false
end if
if mod = 'Y' then
        uo_2.pb_modify.enabled=true
else
        uo_2.pb_modify.enabled=false
end if
if del = 'Y' then
        uo_2.pb_delete.enabled=true
else
        uo_2.pb_delete.enabled=false
end if
if add = 'N' and del = 'N' and mod ='N' then
        uo_2.pb_save.enabled=false
else
        uo_2.pb_save.enabled=true
end if
uf_enable_on_prev input string ucode
string new,mod,del,view
```

```
declare priviledges cursor for
        select privnew,privdel,privmod,privview
        from users
        where ucode = :ucode
        using sqlca;
open priviledges;
fetch priviledges into :new,:del,:mod,:view;
if sqlca.sqlcode <> 0 then
        messagebox("SQL ERROR",sqlca.sqlerrtext)
        close priviledges;
        return
end if
close priviledges;
if new = 'Y' then
        pb_new.enabled = true
        pb_save.enabled = true
end if
if del = 'Y' then
        pb_delete.enabled = true
        pb_save.enabled = true
end if
if mod = 'Y' then
        pb_modify.enabled = true
        pb_save.enabled = true
end if
if view = 'Y' then
        pb_view.enabled = true
end if
uf_register input by ref datawindow a_dw_1
dw_1=a_dw_1
return
uf_setbuttons input Boolean atype
if atype then
        pb_new.visible=false
        pb_save.visible=false
        pb_delete.visible=false
        pb_modify.visible=false
```

```
            pb_view.visible=false
            pb_cancel.visible = false
else
            pb_new.visible=true
            pb_save.visible=true
            pb_delete.visible=true
            pb_modify.visible=true
    pb_view.visible= true
            pb_cancel.visible =true
end if
```

****

Datawindow events:
Dberror event: this will raise the error in case of any
database error:
```
#IF Defined PBNATIVE THEN
return gf_dberror(sqldbcode,sqlerrtext,row,dw_1)
#END IF
```
Itemchanged event:
```
//Most useful code for the datawindow
#IF DEFINED PBWEBFORM THEN
  dw_1.JavaScriptFile = "MyScriptFile.js"
  dw_1.OnClientItemChanged = "MyItemChanged"
  #END IF
#IF DEFINED PBWEBFORM THEN
  dw_1.JavaScriptFile = "MyScriptFile.js"
  dw_1.OnClientItemChanged = "MyItemChanged"
  #END IF
#IF not Defined PBWEBFORM THEN
if trim(data) = "" then
        any nullval
        setnull(nullval)
        dw_1.setitem(row,dw_1.getcolumn(),nullval)
        return 1
end if
string descr
choose case dw_1.describe(dwo.name+".ColType")
```

```
                case "number","decimal(2)","decimal(0)"
                        if isnumber(data) then
                                if real(data) < 0 then
                                gf_message("positive","ERR")
                                        return 2
                                end if
                        else
                        gf_message("number","ERR")
                                return 2
                        end if
end choose
integer count
string colval,filt
choose case i_dml_flag
                case 'N'
        if      dw_1.getcolumn()=    1       AND
Dw_1.describe(dwo.name+".dddw.required")   =   'yes'
then
        if gf_fkeyvalidation(dwo.name,data,dw_1) = 1
then
                gf_messask("Code Already Exists",1)
                return 1
        end if
        END IF
        case 'M','V','D'
        if  dw_1.describe(dwo.name+".dddw.required")
= 'yes' then
        if gf_fkeyvalidation(dwo.name,data,dw_1) = 0
then
                gf_messask("Code Does Not Exist",1)
                return 1
        end if
END IF
end choose
choose case i_dml_flag
        case "M","D","V"
                colname = dwo.name
```

```
                colval = data
                filt = colname +" = '"+colval+"'"
                dw_1.setfilter("")
                dw_1.retrieve(data)
                if dw_1.rowcount() = 0 then
                        gf_message("notfound","ERR")
                        dw_1.insertrow(0)
                        dw_1.scrolltorow(1)
                        return 11
                else
        if i_dml_flag = "D" then
w_mastermenu.sle_1.text  =  "Please  save  to  confirm
delete"
        dw_1.object.datawindow.readonly = true
                else
                        dw_1.settaborder(1,0)
                        end if
                        if i_dml_flag = "V" then
        dw_1.object.datawindow.readonly = true
                        end if
                i_dml_flag = i_dml_flag+"G"
                        end if
end choose
#END IF
```

Code for itemerror event
```
#IF Defined PBNATIVE THEN
        RETURN 1
#END IF
```

Code for ue_dwnprocessenter
```
#IF Defined PBNATIVE THEN
send(handle(this),256,9,long(0,0))
return 1
#END IF
```

Code for user object in the window: used as uo_2
Code for new_event
```
if i_dml_flag = "S" or i_dml_flag = "DG" then
```

```
            datawindowchild dddw
            if dw_1.getcolumn() <> 1 then
                    dw_1.setcolumn(1)
            end if
            dw_1.getchild(dw_1.getcolumnname(),dddw)
            dddw.settransobject(sqlca)
            dddw.retrieve()
end if
i_dml_flag = "N"
cancel_event
if i_dml_flag = "N" or i_dml_flag = "S" then
        dw_1.reset()
end if
uo_2.pb_new.triggerevent("clicked")

pb_view.enabled = true
delete_before_event
if dw_1.modifiedcount() + dw_1.deletedcount() > 0 then
        if      messagebox("UNSAVED       CHANGES!",",
Changes have not been saved ~n Do you wish to
continue?",Question!,YesNo!,2) = 2 then
                messagebox("Information","Please click
the 'Save' Button to ~n Save the changes")
                dw_1.setcolumn(1)
                dw_1.setfocus()
                ts=1
                sle_1.text=" New"
                return 1
        end if
end if

dw_1.modify(dw_1.getitemstring(dw_1.getrow(),1)+".d
ddw.required = no")
choose case i_dml_flag
        case "DG"
                dw_1.object.datawindow.readonly    =
false
```

```
                    dw_1.settaborder(1,10)
        case "MG"
                    dw_1.settaborder(1,10)
end choose
delete_flag = true
sle_1.text = "Delete"
i_dml_flag = "D"

pb_modify.enabled = false
pb_view.enabled = false
pb_delete.enabled = false
modify_before_event
if dw_1.modifiedcount() + dw_1.deletedcount() > 0 then
        if    messagebox("UNSAVED    CHANGES!","
Changes have not been saved ~n Do you wish to
continue?",Question!,YesNo!,2) = 2 then
                    messagebox("Information","Please click
the 'Save' Button to ~n Save the changes")
                    dw_1.setcolumn(1)
                    dw_1.setfocus()
                    ts=1
                    sle_1.text=" New"
                    return 1
        end if
end if

sle_1.text = "Modify"
choose case i_dml_flag
        case "DG"
                    dw_1.object.datawindow.readonly    =
false
                    dw_1.settaborder(1,10)
        case "MG"
                    dw_1.settaborder(1,10)
end choose
if dw_1.rowcount() = 0 then
        dw_1.insertrow(0)
```

```
        dw_1.scrolltorow(dw_1.rowcount())
        dw_1.setfocus()
        dw_1.setcolumn(1)
end if
```

modify_event

```
i_dml_flag = "M"
pb_modify.enabled = false
pb_delete.enabled = false
pb_view.enabled = false
```

code for new_before_event

```
choose case i_dml_flag
        case "V","MG"
if   dw_1.getitemstatus(dw_1.getrow(),0,primary!)   <>
new! Then
        dw_1.reset()
                end if
                dw_1.settaborder(1,10)
        case "DG","VG"
                dw_1.object.datawindow.readonly     =
false
                dw_1.reset()
        case "N"
                if
dw_1.getitemstatus(dw_1.getrow(),0,primary!)  =  new!
then
                        newflag = true
                        return
                else
                        newflag = false
                end if
        case "M","D"
                dw_1.reset()
end choose
if dw_1.getcolumn() <> 1 then
        dw_1.setcolumn(1)
end if
setbuttons(true)
```

```
sle_1.text = " New"
save_before_event
if    i_dml_flag    ="N"    and    dw_1.getitemstatus(
1,0,primary!)=New! then
        return 0
end if
if gf_chkreqcol(dw_1) = 1 then
        update_flag = true
        i_dml_flag = "S"
        dw_1.setitem(1,"usrcd",g_login)
        dw_1.setitem(1,"sysdate",sysdatetime)
else
        update_flag = false
        return
end if
save_event
i_dml_flag = "S"
commit_flag = true
pb_delete.enabled = false
pb_view.enabled = false
pb_modify.enabled = false
view_before_event
if dw_1.modifiedcount() + dw_1.deletedcount() > 0 then
if messagebox("UNSAVED CHANGES!"," Changes have
not been saved ~n Do you wish to continue?",
Question!,YesNo!,2) = 2 then
        messagebox("Information","Please    click    the
'Save' Button to ~n Save the changes")
                dw_1.setcolumn(1)
                dw_1.setfocus()
                ts=1
                sle_1.text-" New"
                return 1
        end if
end if

choose case i_dml_flag
```

```
            case "MG"
                    dw_1.settaborder(1,10)
            case "DG","VG"
                    dw_1.object.datawindow.readonly     =
false
                    dw_1.settaborder(1,10)
end choose
sle_1.text = " View"
i_dml_flag = "V"
view_event
pb_modify.enabled = false
pb_delete.enabled = false
pb_save.enabled = false
pb_view.enabled = false
                            ****
```

Some of the global variables might be needed.

```
string coname,addok, am,fayear,module, machine,loc,
usrname,ghpl_id
date std_date,today
datetime lst_date,fafrdt,fatodt,sysdatetime
int level
long ctr,ref_no
char login
string voutype, ind_pol, corp_pol, pre_auth, claim_reg,
claim_proc, claim_set, mis_rep ,ttype
string   companyname,   company,branch,   ls_string,
gs_fayear, gs_custcd, item_flag
int ts
DataWindow gdw1,gdw2
string gs_which_window
char o_flag,sales,stores,purchase,finance,setup,other
//New for Rk Apex
datawindow dw_x
datawindowchild dwc
string pay,fin,pname,g_logincd,g_login,stype
string chk,subaccd
real amt
```

```
long vouno
string ptype,ins_co,ins_type,contype
```
*****

Second single master window with list option

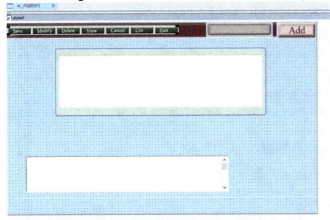

Extra code for List

This list will only work if a datawindow is placed on dw_2
```
if trim(dw_2.dataobject)<>"" then
        dw_2.visible=true
        dw_2.retrieve()
end if
```

quit event:
" "

Event coding same as the user event

List clicked event
```
parent.triggerevent("list")
```
quit clicked event
```
if dw_1.modifiedcount() + dw_1.deletedcount() > 0 then
        if messagebox("Unsaved changes","Changes
have not been saved ~n Do you wish to continue ?
",Question!,YesNo!,1) = 2 then
```

```
                    return
            end if
end if
close (parent)
```

User object for double datawindow

The coding for double datawindow is slightly different
Coding for save button clicked event
//please note the use of dw_2 for second datawindow

```
int rtn
parent.triggerevent("savebefore")
if dw_2.modifiedcount()+dw_2.deletedcount() > 0 then
        if save_flag = true then
                rtn=dw_1.update()
                if rtn <> 1 then
                        gf_messask("Save     Cancelled-
Rolling Back"+ sqlca.sqlerrtext,1)
                        ROLLBACK USING SQLCA;
                        return 1
                else
                        rtn=dw_2.update()
                        if rtn <> 1 then
                        gf_messask("Save     Cancelled-
Rolling Back"+ sqlca.sqlerrtext,1)
                        ROLLBACK USING SQLCA;
                        return 1
                        else

        parent.triggerevent("saveafter")
        if commit_flag = true then
                COMMIT USING SQLCA;

        gf_mess("Additions  /  Changes  have  been
saved")
        dw_2.reset()
```

```
        dw_1.reset()

        pb_cancel.triggerevent("clicked")
        return 0
                                     else
gf_messask("Cancelled-Rolling                    Back"+
sqlca.sqlerrtext,1)
rollback using sqlca;
return 1
        end if
end if
end if
else
        gf_messask("Not Saving",1)
        return 1
end if
else
        dw_2.reset()
        dw_1.reset()
        pb_cancel.triggerevent("clicked")
end if
```

modify clicked event

```
if dw_2.modifiedcount() + dw_2.deletedcount() > 0 then
        if   messagebox("Unsaved   changes","Changes
have not been saved ~n Do you wish to continue ?
",Question!,YesNo!,1) = 2 then
                return
        end if
end if
        dw_1.reset()
        dw_2.reset()
        dw_2.Insertrow(0)
        dw_1.insertrow(0)
dw_1.setcolumn(1)
dw_1.settaborder(1,10)
dw_1.settaborder(2,20)
parent.triggerevent("modify")
```

```
dw_1.setfocus()
```
delete clicked event
```
if dw_2.modifiedcount() + dw_2.deletedcount() > 0 then
if messagebox("Unsaved changes", "Changes have not
been saved ~n Do you wish to continue ? ",
Question!,YesNo!,1) = 2 then
                return
        end if
end if
                dw_1.reset()
                dw_2.reset()
                dw_1.insertrow(0)
                dw_2.insertrow(0)
dw_1.settaborder(1,10)
dw_1.settaborder(2,20)
dw_1.setcolumn(1)

parent.triggerevent("deleted")
dw_1.setfocus()
```
view clicked event
```
if dw_2.modifiedcount() + dw_2.deletedcount() > 0 then
if messagebox("Unsaved changes", "Changes have not
been saved ~n Do you wish to continue ? ",
Question!,YesNo!,1) = 2 then
                return
        end if
end if
                dw_2.reset()
                dw_1.reset()
                dw_2.insertrow(0)
                dw_1.insertrow(0)
dw_1.settaborder(1,10)
dw_1.settaborder(2,20)
dw_1.setcolumn(1)

parent.triggerevent("view")
dw_1.setfocus()
```

cancel clicked event
if dw_2.modifiedcount() + dw_2.deletedcount() > 0 then
        if messagebox("Unsaved changes","Changes have not been saved ~n Do you wish to continue ? ",Question!,YesNo!,1) = 2 then
            return
    end if
end if
          dw_1.reset()
          dw_1.insertrow(0)
          dw_2.insertrow(0)
          dw_2.reset()
dw_1.settaborder(1,10)
dw_1.settaborder(2,20)
dw_1.setcolumn(1)

parent.triggerevent("cancel")
dw_1.setfocus()
quit clicked event
parent.triggerevent("quit")
user object events:
uo_master2 is the name of the userobject
uo_master2 cancel event
dw_1.setfocus()
uo_master2 deleted event
dw_1.setfocus()
uo_master2 modify event
dw_1.setfocus()
uo_master2 quit event
if dw_2.modifiedcount() + dw_2.deletedcount() > 0 then
if messagebox("Unsaved changes","Changes have not been saved ~n Do you wish to continue ? ", Question!,YesNo!,1) = 2 then
            return
    end if
end if
//gf_mess(coname)

close (parent)
uo_master2 view event
dw_1.setfocus()
//all uo_master events can be programmed through windows
window with 2 datawindows Master details window

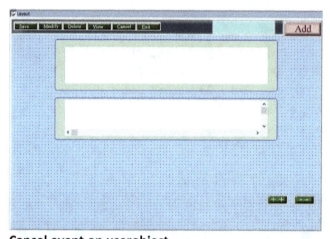

Cancel event on userobject
```
if dw_1.rowcount() = 0 then
        dw_1.insertrow(0)
end if
if dw_2.rowcount()=0 then
        dw_2.insertrow(0)
end if
dw_1.setcolumn(1)
dw_1.setfocus()
uo_1.pb_save.enabled=true
dw_2.Object.DataWindow.ReadOnly="No"
dw_1.Object.DataWindow.ReadOnly="No"
datawindowchild dwchld
dw_1.getchild(dw_1.getcolumnname(),dwchld)
dwchld.settransobject(sqlca)
IF fyok='Y' then
        dwchld.setfilter("fincode = "+string(finyear))
end if
```

```
dwchld.retrieve()
dw_1.setcolumn(2)
dw_1.settaborder(1,0)
dw_1.settaborder(2,10)
dw_1.setfocus()
if addok ='Y' then
flag = 'A'
mle_1.picturename='bgadd.jpg'
else
uo_1.pb_view.triggerevent(clicked!)
end if
```

Deleted event on userobject
```
if dw_1.rowcount() = 0 then
        dw_1.insertrow(0)
end if
if dw_2.rowcount()=0 then
        dw_2.insertrow(0)
end if
dw_1.settaborder(1,10)
dw_1.settaborder(2,20)
dw_1.setcolumn(1)
dw_1.setfocus()
flag = 'D'
dw_2.Object.DataWindow.ReadOnly="No"
dw_1.Object.DataWindow.ReadOnly="No"
mle_1.picturename='bgdelete.jpg'
```
modify event on userobject
```
dw_2.Object.DataWindow.ReadOnly="No"
dw_1.Object.DataWindow.ReadOnly="No"
if dw_1.rowcount() = 0 then
        dw_1.insertrow(0)
end if
if dw_2.rowcount()=0 then
        dw_2.insertrow(0)
end if
dw_1.settaborder(1,10)
dw_1.settaborder(2,20)
```

```
dw_1.setcolumn(1)
dw_1.setfocus()
flag = 'M'
uo_1.pb_save.enabled=true
mle_1.picturename='bgmodify.jpg'
save_after event on userobject
commit_flag = true
save_before event on userobject
int cntr
if flag='DG' then
if gf_messask("Select Option~rDo you Really want to
Delete",2)=1 then
                dw_1.deleterow(1)
        dw_2.rowsmove(1,dw_2.rowcount(),primary!,
dw_2,1,delete!)
                flag="DY"
                if dw_2.rowcount()>0 then
                gf_messask("Not All Data Deleted",1)
                end if
        else
                flag="DN"
        end if
else
//              Delete Last Row if New
                if
dw_2.getitemstatus(dw_2.rowcount(),0,primary!)      =
New! then
dw_2.deleterow(dw_2.rowcount())
end if
                if
dw_2.getitemstatus(dw_2.rowcount(),0,primary!)      =
New! then
        dw_2.deleterow(dw_2.rowcount())
end if
//              Check for Other Blank Rows
        cntr=dw_2.rowcount()
do while cntr>0
```

```
         if dw_2.getitemstatus(cntr,0,primary!) = New! then
                     dw_2.deleterow(cntr)
             end if
                          cntr--
loop
             if gf_chkreqcol(dw_1) = 1 then
                     commit_flag= true
                     save_flag = true
             else
             commit_flag= false
             save_flag = false
             gf_messask("Save Cancelled-Req.Cols",1)
             dw_1.setfocus()
             return 1
             end if
             if gf_chkreqcol(dw_2) = 1 then
                     commit_flag= true
                     save_flag = true
             else
                     commit_flag= false
                     save_flag = false
             gf_messask("Save Cancelled-Req.Cols",1)
                     dw_2.setfocus()
                     return 1
             end if
end if

if left(flag,1)<>'D' then
dw_1.setitem(dw_1.getrow(),"usrcd",g_logincd)
         if fyok='Y' then

         dw_1.setitem(dw_1.getrow(),"fincode",finyear)
         end if
         for ctr=1 to dw_2.rowcount()
                 dw_2.setitem( ctr,"usrcd",g_logincd)
                 if fyok='Y' then
```

```
                dw_2.setitem(ctr,"fincode",finyear)
                        end if
                next
end if
save_flag= true
```
view event on userobject
```
if dw_1.rowcount() = 0 then
        dw_1.insertrow(0)
end if
if dw_2.rowcount()=0 then
        dw_2.insertrow(0)
end if

dw_1.settaborder(1,10)
dw_1.settaborder(2,20)
dw_1.setcolumn(1)
dw_1.setfocus()
flag = 'V'
dw_2.Object.DataWindow.ReadOnly="No"
dw_1.Object.DataWindow.ReadOnly="No"
mle_1.picturename='bgmodify.jpg'
```
Itemchanged event on datawindow 1
```
#IF DEFINED PBWEBFORM THEN
  dw_1.JavaScriptFile = "MyScriptFile.js"
  dw_1.OnClientItemChanged = "MyItemChanged"
  #END IF
#IF DEFINED PBWEBFORM THEN
  dw_1.JavaScriptFile = "MyScriptFile.js"
  dw_1.OnClientItemChanged = "MyItemChanged"
  #END IF

#IF Defined PBNATIVE THEN
er_flag=gf_chkval(
dw_1.describe(dwo.name+".ColType"),data)
if er_flag <> 0 then
        return er_flag
```

```
end if
IF dw_1.getcolumn()<> 1 then
if  dw_1.describe(dwo.name+".dddw.required") = 'yes'
then
if gf_fkeyvalidation(dwo.name,data,dw_1)=0 then
                    er_flag=8
                    return 8
            end if
        end if
end if
if  dw_1.describe(dwo.name+".EDIT.required") = 'yes'
then
                IF trim(data)='' then
                    er_flag=9
                    return 9
                end if
        end if

string colname

colname = dwo.name
choose case flag
        case "M","V","D"
                srno=data
                if trim(srno)= "" then
                        return 1
                end if
                dw_1.SetFilter("")
                if fyok='Y' then
                        if voutype='ST' then

        dw_1.rctricvc(srno,finyear,stype)
                        else
                        dw_1.retrieve(srno,finyear)
                        end if
                else
                        dw_1.retrieve(srno)
```

```
                    end if
                    if dw_1.rowcount() > 0 then
                            dw_1.settaborder(1,0)
                            flag=flag+"G"
                            dw_2.setfilter("")
                            if fyok='Y' then
                                    if voutype="ST" then

dw_2.retrieve(srno,finyear,stype)
                                    else

dw_2.retrieve(srno,finyear)
                                            end if
                            else
                                    dw_2.retrieve(srno)
                    end if
                    if dw_2.rowcount() =0 then
                            dw_2.insertrow(0)
                    else
                            dw_1.settaborder(1,10)
                    end if
                    dw_1.settaborder(1,0)
                    dw_1.setcolumn(2)
                    if flag='DG' then

dw_2.Object.DataWindow.ReadOnly="Yes"

dw_1.Object.DataWindow.ReadOnly="Yes"
                    gf_mess("Please Save to Delete")
                            uo_1.pb_save.setfocus()
                    elseif flag="VG" then

dw_2.Object.DataWindow.ReadOnly="Yes"

dw_1.Object.DataWindow.ReadOnly="Yes"
                    gf_mess("Please Cancel to Cancel")
                            uo_1.pb_save.enabled=false
```

```
                                uo_1.pb_cancel.setfocus()
                    else
                                dw_1.setcolumn(2)
                    end if
                    ELSE
                                dw_1.insertrow(0)
                                RETURN 1
                    end if
end choose
#end if
```

Itemerror event on dw_1
Input: long row, dwobject dwo, string data returns long

```
#IF Defined PBNATIVE THEN
choose case er_flag
        case 1
        gf_messask("Wrong Data Entry Re-Check",1)
        case 2
        gf_messask("Number Should be positive",1)
        case 3
        gf_messask("Number Should be Entered",1)
        case 4
        gf_messask("Not a Date - Re-Enter",1)
        case 5
        gf_messask("Wrong Date -Reenter",1)
        case 6
        gf_messask("Wrong    Date-Date    should    be
between                        "+string(date(fafrdt))+'
'+string(date(fatodt)),1)
        case 7
        gf_messask("Code Already Entered",1)
        case 8
        gf_messask("No. Does not Exist",1)
        case 9
        gf_messask("Column cannot be blank",1)

end choose
```

```
er_flag=0
RETURN 1
#end if
```

Dberror on dw_1
```
#IF Defined PBNATIVE THEN
return gf_dberror(sqldbcode,sqlerrtext,row,dw_1)
#end if
```

Enter event on dw_1
```
#IF Defined PBNATIVE THEN
send(handle(this),256,9,long(0,0))
return 1
#end if
```

Itemchanged event on dw_2
```
#IF DEFINED PBWEBFORM THEN
  dw_2.JavaScriptFile = "MyScriptFile.js"
  dw_2.OnClientItemChanged = "MyItemChanged"
#END IF
#IF DEFINED PBWEBFORM THEN
  dw_2.JavaScriptFile = "MyScriptFile.js"
  dw_2.OnClientItemChanged = "MyItemChanged"
#END IF

#IF Defined PBNATIVE THEN
er_flag=gf_chkval(
dw_2.describe(dwo.name+".ColType"),data)
if er_flag <> 0 then
        return er_flag
end if

if  dw_2.describe(dwo.name+".dddw.required") = 'yes'
then
if gf_fkeyvalidation(dwo.name,data,dw_2) = 0 then
                er_flag=8
                return 8
        end if
    end if
```

```
if  dw_1.describe(dwo.name+".EDIT.required")  =  'yes'
then
                IF trim(data)='' then
                        er_flag=9
                        return 9
                end if
        end if
#end if
```

Remaining events are same as dw_1

Code on ++ button for adding rows in dw_2

```
dw_2.insertrow(0)
dw_2.scrolltorow(dw_2.rowcount())
dw_2.setcolumn(1)
dw_2.setfocus()
```

Code on -- button for adding rows in dw_2

```
int delrow
delrow=dw_2.getrow()
if delrow=1 and dw_2.rowcount()=1 then
        dw_2.deleterow(delrow)
        dw_2.insertrow(0)
elseif delrow=1 and dw_2.rowcount()>1 then
        dw_2.scrollnextrow()
        dw_2.deleterow(delrow)
elseif delrow=dw_2.rowcount() then
        dw_2.scrollpriorrow()
        dw_2.deleterow(delrow)
else
        dw_2.scrollnextrow()
        dw_2.deleterow(delrow)
end if
dw_2.setcolumn(1)
dw_2.setfocus()
```

opening event for window

```
w_mastermenu.sle_1.enabled=true
w_mastermenu.sle_1.text=pb_name.text+"      Opening
Please Wait"
w_mastermenu.pb_1.enabled=false
```

```
this.title=pb_name.text
uo_1.uf_reg(dw_1,dw_2)
dw_1.settransobject(sqlca)
dw_2.settransobject(sqlca)
dw_1.reset()
dw_2.reset()
dw_1.insertrow(0)
dw_2.insertrow(0)
dw_1.setcolumn(1)
dw_1.setfocus()
flag='A'
wf_enable()
dw_2.setrowfocusindicator(hand!)
this.x=0
this.y=0
this.width=3657
this.height=1992
uo_1.pb_cancel.triggerevent(clicked!)
if left(coname,1)='S' then
        this.icon="backup.ico"
else
        this.icon="tomcat.ico"
end if
dw_1.modify("datawindow.color='"+
string(rgb(216,228,248))+"'")
r_1.fillcolor=rgb(216,228,248)
dw_2.modify("datawindow.color='"+
string(rgb(216,228,248))+"'")
r_2.fillcolor=rgb(216,228,248)
```

Report windows

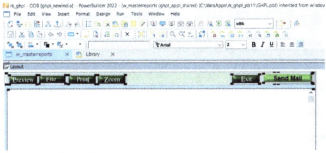

Preview clicked

```
sle_2.text = "Preview"
long lrows
lrows = dw_1.retrieve(companyname)
if lrows = 0 then
        messagebox("Information","No  details  exist  .  .
.")
        return
end if
```

file clicked event

```
sle_2.text = " To File"
dw_1.saveas("",Excel5!,true)
w_mastermenu.sle_1.text = "To Preview the details.."
```

print clicked event

```
sle_2.text = "  Print"
s_prnset l_prnset
l_prnset.dw_a = dw_1
l_prnset.default = 1
openwithparm(w_prnset,l_prnset)
```

zoom clicked

```
openwithparm(w_zoom,dw_1)
```

w_prnset used in report print

Open event

```
s_prnset l_prnset
```

```
l_prnset = message.powerobjectparm
if not isnull(l_prnset.default) then
        wf_assigndw(l_prnset.dw_a)
        ddlb_size.selectitem(l_prnset.default)
else
        wf_assigndw(l_prnset.dw_a)
        ddlb_size.selectitem(1)
end if
if LeftA(coname,1)='S' then
        this.icon="backup.ico"
else
        this.icon="tomcat.ico"
end if
```

close event

```
string range,status,str1
if okcancel = "Y" then
        if rb_pages.checked = true then
                range = sle_range.text
                str1 = "datawindow.print.page.range =
'"+range+"'"
                status = dw_a.modify(str1)
                if status <> "" then

        messagebox("MODIFY",""+status+" Unable   to
modify datawindow properties")
                end if
        end if
        for ctr=1 to long(copy.text)
                dw_a.print()
        next
end if
```

ok clicked event

```
okcancel = "Y"
close(parent)
```

setup clicked event

```
PrintSetup()
```

Cancel clicked event

```
okcancel = "N"
close(parent)
```
Zoom window used in printing

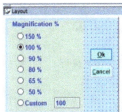

Open event in w_zoom
```
dw_x = message.powerobjectparm
zoom = 100
if LeftA(coname,1)='S' then
        this.icon="backup.ico"
else
        this.icon="tomcat.ico"
end if
```
close event in zoom
```
string status
status = dw_x.modify("datawindow.print.preview.zoom
= "+string(zoom))
status     =     dw_x.modify("datawindow.zoom     =
"+string(zoom))
if status <> "" then
        messagebox("MODIFY","Unable     to     modify
datawindow properties")
end if
```
ok clicked event
```
okcancel = "Y"
close(parent)
```
cancel clicked
```
okcancel = "N"
close(parent)
```
selecting zoom option
```
zoom = 100
sle_1.text='100'
cb_1.triggerevent(clicked!)
```

same for other options
sle_1 %entry modified event
zoom = integer(sle_1.text)
cb_1.triggerevent(clicked!)
Report window with 2nd datawindow for report options

Dw_2 item error
return 1
preview button clicked
dw_2.accepttext()
Remaining same as report 1
Coding for selection on dw_2 written on the report
****

The following are the some of the global functions used in the masters:
Code for gf_dberror
// input, interger sqldbcode, string sqlerrtext, integer row, datawindow //dw_b, this event is raised automatically.
int li_filename
if sqldbcode <> 0 then
          messagebox("Database Error",sqlerrtext,stopsign!)
          dw_b.scrolltorow(row)
          return 1
          li_filename   =
fileopen("\\ntserver\e\newerror.log",   linemode!, Write!, shared!, append!)
          if li_filename > 0 then

```
            if          filewrite(li_filename,"~n~r"+"
"+string(today())+ " " +string(now())+&
                                    "Code:           "
+string(sqldbcode) + "Message :" + sqlerrtext)  < 0 then
                    messagebox("Error  Log  Failure
", "Unable to Log this Error ")
                    filewrite(li_filename,' ')
          end if
          if fileclose(li_filename) < 0 then
                    messagebox("Error  Log  Failure
", "Unable to close Log File ")
          end if
     else
     messagebox("Error  Log  Failure  ", "Unable  to
Open Log Error File ")
     end if
end if
return 0
```

This useful when we have huge data to share with dropdowns in multiple datawindows

```
dwc_share input by ref datawindow, string colname
returns none
if        w_mastermenu.dw_1.rowcount()=0          then
w_mastermenu.dw_1.retrieve()
dwno.getchild(colname,dwc)
dwc.settransobject(sqlca)
dwc.setfilter("")
dwc.filter()
w_mastermenu.dw_1.sharedata(dwc)
```

dwf_dwcfiltret   input   datawindow   dwno,string colname,string filter returns none

//filter a datawindow dropdown as a childdatawindow

```
dwno.getchild(colname,dwc)
dwc.settransobject(sqlca)
dwc.setfilter(filter)
dwc.retrieve()
```

dwf_dwcfiltset input datawindow dwno,string colname,string filter returns none
//sets the filter too
dwno.getchild(colname,dwc)
dwc.settransobject(sqlca)
dwc.setfilter(filter)
dwc.filter()
dwf_rvmb input datawindow dwno
//to check and inform no data retrieved
ctr = dwno.rowcount()
if ctr = 0 then
        messagebox("Information","There is no output for the criteria you have choosen")
end if
// Function f_mail_error_to_string (string a_MailReturnCode, string a_Display) returns string
// where: a_MailReturnCode
        MailReturnCode value
//a_Message   Error message to prepend to return string
//a_Display   Boolean   (TRUE=display error messagebox)

string   s

choose case a_MailReturnCode
        case mailReturnAccessDenied!
                s = 'Access Denied'
        case mailReturnAttachmentNotFound!
                s = 'Attachment Not Found'
        case mailReturnAttachmentOpenFailure!
                s = 'Attachment Open Failure'
        case mailReturnAttachmentWriteFailure!
                s = 'Attachment Write Failure'
        case mailReturnDiskFull!
                s = 'Disk Full'
        case mailReturnFailure!

```
                s = 'Failure'
        case mailReturnInsufficientMemory!
                s = 'Insufficient Memory'
        case mailReturnInvalidMessage!
                s = 'Invalid Message'
        case mailReturnLoginFailure!
                s = 'Login Failure'
        case mailReturnMessageInUse!
                s = 'Message In Use'
        case mailReturnNoMessages!
                s = 'No Messages'
        case mailReturnSuccess!
                s = 'Success'
        case mailReturnTextTooLarge!
                s = 'Text Too Large'
        case mailReturnTooManyFiles!
                s = 'Too Many Files'
        case mailReturnTooManyRecipients!
                s = 'Too Many Recipients'
        case mailReturnTooManySessions!
                s = 'Too Many Sessions'
        case mailReturnUnknownRecipient!
                s = 'Unknown Recipient'
        case mailReturnUserAbort!
                s = 'User Abort'

        case else
                s = 'Other'
end choose

if a_Display then MessageBox ( 'Mail Return Code',
a_Message + ' ' + s, Exclamation!)

return s
gf_chkreqcol input datawindow dw_control returns
integer
integer li_colnbr = 1
```

```
long ll_row = 1
string ls_colname, ls_textname,dw_name
IF dw_control.AcceptText() = -1 THEN
        dw_control.SetFocus()
        RETURN -2
END IF
IF dw_control.FindRequired( Primary!, ll_row,  &
        li_colnbr, ls_colname, false ) < 0 THEN
        RETURN -2
END IF
IF ll_row <> 0 THEN
//      ls_textname = ls_colname + "_t.Text"
//      ls_colname = dw_control.Describe(ls_textname)
if string(dw_control)="dw_1" then
        dw_name="Header"
elseif string(dw_control)="dw_2" then
        dw_name="Details"
else
        dw_name="others"
end if
MessageBox("Required Value Missing", "Please enter
Data for:"       +dw_name+",Col:"   +ls_colname+    ",
Row: "+ String(ll_row) + ".",StopSign! )
        dw_control.SetColumn(li_colnbr)
        dw_control.ScrollToRow(ll_row)
        dw_control.SetFocus()
        RETURN -1
END IF
RETURN 1
```

Gf_chkval input string coltypes, string datas returns integer

```
integer li_colnbr = 1
long ll_row = 1
string ls_colname, ls_textname,dw_name
IF dw_control.AcceptText() = -1 THEN
        dw_control.SetFocus()
        RETURN -2
```

```
END IF
IF dw_control.FindRequired( Primary!, ll_row, &
        li_colnbr, ls_colname, false ) < 0 THEN
        RETURN -2
END IF
IF ll_row <> 0 THEN
//      ls_textname = ls_colname + "_t.Text"
//      ls_colname = dw_control.Describe(ls_textname)
if string(dw_control)="dw_1" then
        dw_name="Header"
elseif string(dw_control)="dw_2" then
        dw_name="Details"
else
        dw_name="others"
end if
        MessageBox("Required Value Missing", "Please
enter Data for:"+dw_name+",Col:"   +ls_colname+    ",
Row: "+ String(ll_row) + ".",StopSign! )
        dw_control.SetColumn(li_colnbr)
        dw_control.ScrollToRow(ll_row)
        dw_control.SetFocus()
        RETURN -1
END IF
RETURN 1
Gf_chkval_null input string coltypes, string datas,
returns integer
integer li_colnbr = 1
long ll_row = 1
string ls_colname, ls_textname,dw_name
IF dw_control.AcceptText() = -1 THEN
        dw_control.SetFocus()
        RETURN -2
END IF
IF dw_control.FindRequired( Primary!, ll_row, &
        li_colnbr, ls_colname, false ) < 0 THEN
        RETURN -2
END IF
```

```
IF ll_row <> 0 THEN
//      ls_textname = ls_colname + "_t.Text"
//      ls_colname = dw_control.Describe(ls_textname)
if string(dw_control)="dw_1" then
        dw_name="Header"
elseif string(dw_control)="dw_2" then
        dw_name="Details"
else
        dw_name="others"
end if
MessageBox("Required Value Missing", "Please enter
Data for:"      +dw_name+",Col:"   +ls_colname+   ",
Row: "+ String(ll_row) + ".",StopSign! )
        dw_control.SetColumn(li_colnbr)
        dw_control.ScrollToRow(ll_row)
        dw_control.SetFocus()
        RETURN -1
END IF
RETURN 1
```
Gf_deletedata input nobe,returns none
```
//to save deleted data in a table for audit purpose
long srno
datetime dt
dt=datetime(today())
SELECT max(deletedata.srno  )    INTO :srno     FROM
deletedata ;
srno++
 INSERT INTO deletedata
        ( srno,    ref_no,        ghpl_id,        ttype,
usrcd,       sysdate )
 VALUES ( :srno,      :ref_no,     :ghpl_id,      :ttype,
:g_logincd,    :dt ) ;
 if sqlca.sqlcode<>0 then
        gf_messask(sqlca.sqlerrtext,1)
end if
return sqlca.sqlcode
```
gf_facheckdate input date returns integer

```
if chkdate < date(fafrdt) or chkdate > date(fatodt) then
//      gf_messask("Wrong    Date-Date    should    be
between                 "+string(date(fafrdt))+'              &
'+string(date(fatodt)),1)
        return 6
else
        return 0
end if
        return 0


gf_facheckdt input date return integer

if chkdate < fafrdt or chkdate > fatodt then
//to check date entered is not out of range
//      gf_messask("Wrong    Date-Date    should    be
between                           "+string(date(fafrdt))+'
'+string(date(fatodt)),1)
        return 6
else
        return 0
end if
        return 1
```
**gf_fkeyvalidation input string colname, string colval,
datawindow which_dw**
```
which_dw.getchild(colname,dwc)
colval=trim(colval)
ctr=              dwc.find(colname+"              =
'"+colval+"'",1,dwc.rowcount())
if ctr= 0 then
        return 0  // row not found
elseif ctr>0 then
        return 1  // row found
elseif ctr<0 then
ctr= dwc.find("code = '"+colval+"'",1,dwc.rowcount())
if ctr= 0 then
        return 0  // row not found
else
```

```
                return 1   // row found
end if
end if
return 0
```

Gf_nextyear input date returns date

```
date todate
todate=date(string(year(frdate)+1)+'/'+
string(month(frdate))+'/'+string(day(frdate)))
todate=relativedate(todate,-1)
return todate
```

gf_mess input string mess return none
//to set message on the messagebar

```
if      w_mastermenu.sle_1.enabled=false      then
w_mastermenu.sle_1.enabled=true
w_mastermenu.sle_1.text=mess
```

gf_message input string cols, string flags returns none
//to set message on the message about the col

```
if      w_mastermenu.sle_1.enabled=false      then
w_mastermenu.sle_1.enabled=true
string desc
  SELECT descrip
   INTO :desc
   FROM message
  WHERE col = :col   ;
        if sqlca.sqlcode = 100 then
                desc=upper(col)
                end if
        choose case flags
                case "MG"

        w_mastermenu.sle_1.text='Please      Change
'+desc
                case ELSE
                        w_mastermenu.sle_1.text
='Please Enter '+desc
                end choose
                return
```

gf_messask input string mess, integer ask returns integer
int retval
if trim(mess)="" then
        mess="? message"+mess
end if
choose case ask
case 1
        messagebox("Message",mess,Exclamation!)
        retval = 0
case 2
        retval   =
        messagebox("Message",mess,Question!,YesNo!
,1)
case 3
        retval   =
        messagebox("Message",mess,Question!,
YesNoCancel!,2)
case 4
        retval   =   messagebox("Message",mess,
        Question!,YesNo!,2)
end choose
return retval

gf_messask_no input string mess, integer ask returns integer
int retval
if trim(mess)="" then
        mess="? message"+mess
end if
choose case ask
        case 1

        messagebox("Message",mess,Exclamation!)
                retval = 0
        case 2

```
                retval                              =
        messagebox("Message",mess,Question!,YesNo!
,2)
        case 3
                retval                              =
        messagebox("Message",mess,Question!,YesNoC
ancel!,2)
        case 4
                retval                              =
        messagebox("Message",mess,Question!,YesNo!
,2)
        end choose
                        return retval
```

gf_modifydata input none return integer

```
long srno
datetime dt
dt=datetime(today())
        SELECT max(srno  )    INTO :srno      FROM
modifydata ;
srno++
 INSERT INTO modifydata
    ( srno,        ref_no,        ghpl_id,        ttype,
usrcd,        sysdate )
  VALUES ( :srno,    :ref_no,      :ghpl_id,      :ttype,
:g_logincd,    :dt ) ;
  if sqlca.sqlcode<>0 then
        gf_messask(sqlca.sqlerrtext,1)
end if
return sqlca.sqlcode
```

gf_numbertowords input decimal xcv_net, returns string

```
string cnum,camt,ones,teen,tens
if xcv_net>99999999 then
return ""
end if
camt=""
```

```
ones= 'ONE  TWO THREE FOUR FIVE SIX SEVENEIGHT
NINE '
teen= 'TEN ELEVEN   TWELVE   THIRTEEN FOURTEEN
FIFTEEN SIXTEEN SEVENTEEN EIGHTEEN NINETEEN'
tens=  'TWENTY  THIRTY  FORTY    FIFTY    SIXTY
SEVENTYEIGHTY NINETY'
cnum=LeftA(string(long(xcv_net)),8)
cnum=space(8 -LenA(cnum))+cnum
IF LeftA(cnum,1)>' ' then
camt=
righttrim(MidA(ones,long(LeftA(cnum,1))*5+1,5))+'
CRORES '
end if
IF LeftA(cnum,3)>'  ' then
if MidA(cnum,2,1)>'1' then

camt=camt+righttrim(MidA(tens,long(MidA(cnum,2,1))
*7 -13,7))
  IF MidA(cnum,3,1)>' ' then
    camt=camt+'
'+righttrim(MidA(ones,long(MidA(cnum,3,1))*5+1,5))
   end if
   camt = camt+' LAKHS '
elseif MidA(cnum,2,1)= '1' then
   camt=
camt+righttrim(MidA(teen,long(MidA(cnum,3,1))*9+1,9
))+' LAKHS '
elseif MidA(cnum,2,2)= '00' then
   camt= camt
elseif MidA(cnum,3,1)> '0' then
   camt=
camt+righttrim(MidA(ones,long(MidA(cnum,3,1))*5+1,5
))+' LAKHS '
END if
end if

cnum=MidA(cnum,3,6)
```

```
IF LeftA(cnum,3)>' ' then
if MidA(cnum,2,1)>'1' then

camt=camt+righttrim(MidA(tens,long(MidA(cnum,2,1))
*7 -13,7))
  IF MidA(cnum,3,1)>' ' then
    camt=camt+'
'+righttrim(MidA(ones,long(MidA(cnum,3,1))*5+1,5))
  end if
  camt = camt+' THOUSAND '
elseif MidA(cnum,2,1)= '1' then
  camt=
camt+righttrim(MidA(teen,long(MidA(cnum,3,1))*9+1,9
))+' THOUSAND '
elseif MidA(cnum,2,2)= '00' then
  camt= camt
elseif MidA(cnum,3,1)> '0' then
  camt=
camt+righttrim(MidA(ones,long(MidA(cnum,3,1))*5+1,5
))+' THOUSAND '
END if
end if
IF MidA(cnum,4,1)>'0' then
camt=camt+righttrim(MidA(ones,long(MidA(cnum,4,1))
*5+1,5))+ ' HUNDRED '
end if
if MidA(cnum,5,1)>'1' then
camt                                              =
camt+righttrim(MidA(tens,long(MidA(cnum,5,1))*7    -
13,7))
IF RightA(cnum,1)>'0' then
  camt=                                      camt+'
'+righttrim(MidA(ones,long(RightA(cnum,1))*5+1,5))
end if
elseif MidA(cnum,5,1)='1' then
```

```
camt=camt+righttrim(MidA(teen,long(RightA(cnum,1))*
9+1,9))
else
camt=camt+righttrim(MidA(ones,long(RightA(cnum,1))*
5+1,5))
END if
//Paise Checking
cnum=RightA(string(round(xcv_net,2)),9)
cnum=space(9 -LenA(cnum))+cnum

if RightA(cnum,2)<>'00' then
camt=camt+ " AND PAISE "
//*check tens and ones for paise
  if MidA(cnum,8,1)>'1' then
camt                                              =
camt+righttrim(MidA(tens,long(MidA(cnum,8,1))*7      -
13,7))
  if RightA(cnum,1)>'0' then
camt=                                       camt+'
'+righttrim(MidA(ones,long(RightA(cnum,1))*5+1,5))
end if
elseif MidA(cnum,8,1)='1' then
camt=camt+righttrim(MidA(teen,long(RightA(cnum,1))*
9+1,9))
elseif RightA(cnum,2)= '00' then
camt= camt+'ZERO'
else
CAMT=CAMT+righttrim(MidA(ONES,long(RightA(CNUM,
1))*5+1,5))
END if
end if
camt="RUPEES "+camt+' ONLY'
RETURN trim(camt)
Gf_pass input string pass returns string
int leng,ascd
string passout
passout=""
```

```
leng=Len(pass)
for ctr = 1 to leng
        ascd=Asc(Mid(pass,ctr,1))
        if ascd >127 then
                ascd -=127
        else
                ascd+=127
        end if
        passout=passout+Char(ascd)
next
return passout
```

gf_setfilter input datawindow dwno, string colname, string filter, returns none

```
dwno.getchild(colname,dwc)
dwc.settransobject(sqlca)
dwc.setfilter(filter)
dwc.filter()
```

gf_smsdata input string ph_no, strin sms_mess returns integer

//to store the message in smstable to be sent later

```
datetime dt
long sno
dt=datetime(today())
if isnull(ph_no) or len(ph_no)<10 then
        return -1
else
        select    max(sno)    into    :sno    from combidata.dbo.sms_data ;
        sno=sno+1
INSERT        INTO        combidata.dbo.sms_data
(sms_mess,ph_no,active,usrcd,sysdate,sno)
values(:sms_mess,:ph_no,1,:g_logincd,:dt,:sno);
 gf_messask(sqlca.sqlerrtext,1)
return sqlca.sqlcode
end if
```

gf_syserror input none, output none

```
messagebox("Error      in      Apex      -      Error
Num:"+string(error.number)," message:"+error.text+'
For '+error.windowmenu+' In '+error.objectevent)
int li_filename
li_filename=fileopen("\\ghplserver\sqlbackup\error.log
",linemode!,write!,shared!,append!)
if li_filename>0 then
        filewrite(li_filename,"Error inApplication - Error
Num:"+string(error.number)+" message:"+error.text+"
where:"+error.windowmenu+" Object:"+error.object+"
event:"+error.objectevent+" Line:"+string(error.line)+"
Dt/Tm:"+string(today())+' '+string(now()))
        filewrite(li_filename," ")
end if
fileclose(li_filename)
gf_verifydt input date xdate, returns integer
if xdate >std_date or xdate <= today() then
        return 0
else
        return 5
end if
return 0
s_prnset input datawindow dw_a,double default
//structure for printer set to be sent to printer window
```

PART 2
Develop Application using Master windows

Chapter 1
TPA Software

Let us take a case where we have to start from scratch. I will take an example of the Health Insurance TPA I worked on from scratch. They were not using any software, except using Excel for saving some data.

First, I will explain the processes. There are two processes individual policies and corporate or group policies. Individual policies contain single-person details. Name, age, amount insured, and address of the person. These individuals are issued a single ID card with a photo, name, age, amount, and insurance company, and these are printed on preprinted label paper with the TPA name and address, telephone nos, etc. The first thing we have to do is feed the individual data and attach a photo to his data. When we enter a certain no of data, we can print it on the label paper. Then the labels are cut and stacked then these will be sent to the addresses. The same way the address labels are printed. One thing I found after seeing the individual data are they are not so individual, each individual may have dependents like spouse, sons and daughters, parents, brothers and sisters. Each will share the same address. We decided to use the Head and details scheme for entering data. The main members' data is entered on the header and address. In the details section each individual name, age, relation, and amount are entered. These header and details data are linked with a single id or number. The detailed data is entered in serial nos. The photos are stored in a server with the linking id. So, when printing labels the photos are picked from the server and printed.

The same principle is used for corporate policies. Here corporate details are entered in a separate table and linked when data is entered. The header will contain the corporate code, individual/employee name, employee

ID, and policy amount. Here is mostly an amount allotted for each employee which will be for all the members of the family. Sometimes a floating amount is also allotted for the corporation. Which can be used when the individual amount is used fully. Here same way data is entered photos stored and labels printed. Here the printed IDs are sent to the corporate office.

I have not prepared any documents and worked on the application as it was brought to me. I worked on the development and maintenance part for around 4 to 5 years as there were changes in the requirements as brought by adding other insurance companies or requirements by the existing insurance companies.

First, we need to prepare SQL tables.

Let us see what the table structure for Hospital Master Table, then we will see how to make datawindow and attach it to a window and run without adding any more code.

```
CREATE TABLE dbo.hospitals (hs_cd varchar(5) NOT
NULL , hs_name varchar(80) NOT NULL , co_add1
varchar(30) NOT NULL , co_add2 varchar(30) , co_add3
varchar(30) , city varchar(4) NOT NULL , pincode
varchar(10) , usrcd varchar(5) NOT NULL , sysdate
datetime NOT NULL , hs_gr varchar(5) , bankacno
varchar(30) , bankname varchar(50) , bankcity
varchar(30) , hs_type char(1) , nims_tariff char(1) ,
reg_no varchar(50) , pan_no varchar(50) , grade char(1)
, email varchar(50) , actype varchar(20) , ifsc_code
varchar(50) , branch_code varchar(50) , discount
varchar(10) , micr varchar(15) , tan_no varchar(20) ,
chq_name varchar(50) , tds_ys char(1) , tds_date
smalldatetime , tds_prc numeric(5,2) , serv_tax_no
varchar(30) , ph_no varchar(10) , ppn_type char(1) ,
nia_code varchar(30) , CONSTRAINT hospitals_cd
PRIMARY KEY (hs_cd)) ;
```

Datawindow Query:

SELECT hospitals.hs_cd, hospitals.hs_name,
hospitals.co_add1, hospitals.co_add2,
hospitals.co_add3, hospitals.city,
hospitals.pincode, hospitals.usrcd,
hospitals.sysdate, hospitals.hs_gr,
hospitals.bankacno, hospitals.bankname,
hospitals.bankcity, hospitals.hs_type,
hospitals.nims_tariff, hospitals.reg_no,
hospitals.pan_no, hospitals.grade,
hospitals.email, hospitals.actype,
hospitals.ifsc_code, hospitals.branch_code,
hospitals.discount, hospitals.micr,
hospitals.tan_no, hospitals.chq_name,
hospitals.tds_ys, hospitals.tds_date,
hospitals.tds_prc, hospitals.serv_tax_no,
hospitals.ph_no, hospitals.ppn_type,
hospitals.nia_code
FROM hospitals
WHERE hospitals.hs_cd = :cd

Create a datawindow in Freeform with the above sql query and add cd string as a retrieval argument.

Create another datawindow with the above query without the where clause in either Grid or Tabular form.

Save them and put the first one on dw_1 and the second one on dw_2 using master with 2 datawindows with list option.

You can add the window to the menu and can check. The Window will run without any further code.

The window code, convertible to window:

```
forward
global type w_hospitals from w_master1
end type
end forward


global type w_hospitals from w_master1
integer width = 3653
integer height = 2268
end type
global w_hospitals w_hospitals
type variables
int olevel
end variables
on w_hospitals.create
int iCurrent
call super::create
end on
on w_hospitals.destroy
call super::destroy
end on
event open;call super::open;choose case  g_login
        case 'SH','DL','JY','PS','00'
                olevel=level
                level=0
        case    else
                module='xxx'
                level=3
END choose
end event
event close;call super::close;level=olevel
this.height=520
```

```
end event
type pb_name from w_master1`pb_name within
w_hospitals
string text = "Hospitals"
end type
type mle_1 from w_master1`mle_1 within w_hospitals
integer width = 471
integer height = 172
end type
type uo_1 from w_master1`uo_1 within w_hospitals
end type
event uo_1::cancel;call super::cancel;dw_2.visible=true
dw_2.retrieve()
dw_1.settaborder("tds_date",0)
end event
event uo_1::modify;call super::modify
end event
type dw_2 from w_master1`dw_2 within w_hospitals
boolean visible = true
integer x = 9
integer y = 1652
integer width = 3621
integer height = 520
string dataobject = "dd_hosp_list"
boolean hscrollbar = true
boolean vscrollbar = false
end type
type dw_1 from w_master1`dw_1 within w_hospitals
integer x = 78
integer y = 176
integer width = 3515
integer height = 1432
string dataobject = "d_hospitals"
end type
event                    dw_1::itemchanged;call
super::itemchanged;er_flag  =  super::  event
itemchanged(row,dwo,data)
```

```
choose case er_flag
        case 0
        case else
                return 1
end choose
string tds_ys
choose case dwo.name
        case "co_cd"
                dw_1.getchild("co_reg_cd",dwc)
                dwc.settransobject(sqlca)
                dwc.setfilter("co_cd='"+data+"'")
                dwc.filter()
        case "tds_ys"
                if data='N' then

        dw_1.settaborder("tds_date",260)
                else
                        dw_1.settaborder("tds_date",0)
                end if
end choose
if flag='MG' then
        tds_ys=dw_1.getitemstring(row,"tds_ys")
                        if tds_ys='N' then
        dw_1.settaborder("tds_date",260)
                else
                        dw_1.settaborder("tds_date",0)
                end if
end if
end event
event   dw_1::editchanged;call   super::editchanged;if
dwo.name='hs_name' then
dw_2.setfilter("hs_name like '"+ data+"%'")
dw_2.filter()
end if
end event
type sle_1 from w_master1`sle_1 within w_hospitals
end type
```

type rr_1 from w_master1`rr_1 within w_hospitals
integer x = 41
integer y = 168
integer width = 3589
integer height = 1468
end type

****

Let us look at the individual policy table structures
Header common for a family policy

```
TABLE Individual_policy_head(
        ref_no numeric(19, 0) NOT NULL, unique no
        policy_no varchar(25) NOT NULL, policy no
issued by the insurance company
        prev_policy_no   varchar(25)    NULL,    if
renewal policy previous policy for reference
        policy_from   smalldatetime   NOT   NULL,
starting date
        policy_to smalldatetime NOT NULL, ending
data
        insured_name  varchar(40)   NOT  NULL,  the
person who took the policy
        add1 varchar(40) NOT NULL, address
        add2 varchar(40) NULL,
        add3 varchar(40) NULL,
        city varchar(5) NOT NULL,
        pincode varchar(10) NULL,
        net_premium  numeric(10,  2)  NOT  NULL,
premium after deducting the service tax, based
on which service charges are calculated
        service_tax numeric(10, 2) NOT NULL, paid
to the govt.
        decl_date    datetime    NULL,   when   the
declaration given
        ins_co  varchar(5)  NOT  NULL,  insurance
company
        ins_reg  varchar(5)  NOT  NULL,  regional
office
        ins_branch  varchar(5)  NOT  NULL,  branch
office
        usrcd varchar(5) NOT NULL, the user who
changed the data last
        sysdate  smalldatetime  NOT  NULL,  date  of
entry and modified
```

```
        tpa_id varchar(20) NOT NULL, id generated
for tpa reference partial no.
        disp_date    smalldatetime    NULL,    ids
dispatched date
        pol_type varchar(5) NULL, type of policy-
individual or group
        remarks varchar(100) NULL,
        agentcd varchar(20) NULL,
        entry_dt  smalldatetime  NULL,  date  of
entry
        finyear tinyint NOT NULL, financial year
        sum_insured numeric(18, 0) NULL,
        password varchar(10) NULL, user password
        dev_officer varchar(20) NULL,
        pod varchar(20) NULL, delivery report
        pol_payment varchar(10) NULL,
        opt_64vb char(1) NULL,
        phc_cd varchar(20) NULL,
        pr_code varchar(5) NULL,
 CONSTRAINT     POLICY_HEAD_CD     PRIMARY     KEY
NONCLUSTERED
(
        ref_no ASC,
        finyear ASC
)WITH (PAD_INDEX = OFF, STATISTICS_NORECOMPUTE =
OFF, IGNORE_DUP_KEY = OFF, ALLOW_ROW_LOCKS = ON,
ALLOW_PAGE_LOCKS  =  ON,  FILLFACTOR  =  90)  ON
PRIMARY
) ON PRIMARY
```

Details of each member of the family

```
TABLE Individual_policy_det(
        ref_no numeric(19, 0) NOT NULL,
        slno tinyint NOT NULL,
        tpa_id varchar(20) NOT NULL,
        name_insured varchar(50) NOT NULL,
        age tinyint NOT NULL,
        sex char(1) NOT NULL,
        occupation varchar(50) NOT NULL,
        relation varchar(50) NOT NULL,
        sum_insured numeric(10, 0) NULL,
        bonus_amount  numeric(10,  0)  NOT  NULL,
accumulated bonus
        bal_amount  numeric(10,  0)  NOT  NULL,
balance of sum insured+ bonus- utilised amt
        remarks varchar(500) NOT NULL,
```

```sql
        usrcd    varchar(5)   NULL,   the   user   who
entered or modified the data
        sysdate datetime NULL, date of entry of
modification
        cum_prc numeric(5, 2) NULL, bonus detils
        sum_ins1 numeric(18, 0) NULL,
        cum_prc1 numeric(18, 0) NULL,
        bon_amt1 numeric(18, 0) NULL,
        sum_ins2 numeric(18, 0) NULL,
        cum_prc2 numeric(18, 0) NULL,
        bon_amt2 numeric(18, 0) NULL,
        dom_hosp numeric(18, 0) NULL, domiciliary
hospitalisation amount authorised
        photo_path varchar(50) NOT NULL, path of
the saved photo
        photo_ys char(1) NULL, photo received or
not
        finyear tinyint NOT NULL,
        end_date smalldatetime NULL,
        premium numeric(5, 0) NULL,
        pol_type varchar(5) NULL,
        sum_ins3 numeric(18, 0) NULL,
        cum_prc3 numeric(5, 0) NULL,
        bon_amt3 numeric(10, 0) NULL,
        sum_ins4 numeric(18, 0) NULL,
        cum_prc4 numeric(5, 0) NULL,
        bon_amt4 numeric(10, 0) NULL,
        sum_ins5 numeric(18, 0) NULL,
        cum_prc5 numeric(5, 0) NULL,
        bon_amt5 numeric(10, 0) NULL,
        dob smalldatetime NULL,
        membercode varchar(20) NULL,
        csemp_no varchar(30) NULL,
        cssl_no varchar(10) NULL,
 CONSTRAINT policy_det_cds PRIMARY KEY CLUSTERED
(
        ref_no ASC,
        slno ASC,
        finyear ASC
)WITH (PAD_INDEX = OFF, STATISTICS_NORECOMPUTE =
OFF, IGNORE_DUP_KEY = OFF, ALLOW_ROW_LOCKS = ON,
ALLOW_PAGE_LOCKS  =  ON,  FILLFACTOR  =  90)  ON
PRIMARY
) ON PRIMARY
```

The data entry screens for these entries: some part of the details screen is hidden here.

Query for the dw_1 datawindow
SELECT policy_head.ref_no,   policy_head.policy_no,
    policy_head.policy_from,   policy_head.policy_to,
    policy_head.insured_name, policy_head.add1,
    policy_head.add2,   policy_head.add3,
    policy_head.city,   policy_head.pincode,
policy_head.prev_policy_no, policy_head.net_premium,
policy_head.service_tax,   policy_head.decl_date,
  policy_head.ins_co, policy_head.ins_reg,
policy_head.ins_branch,   policy_head.usrcd,
        policy_head.sysdate,   policy_head.ghpl_id,
policy_head.disp_date,   policy_head.pol_type,
policy_head.remarks,   policy_head.agentcd,
policy_head.entry_dt,   policy_head.finyear,
policy_address.bank_name, policy_address.bank_acno,
policy_address.bank_city, policy_head.sum_insured,
policy_address.izone,   policy_head.dev_officer,
policy_head.pod,   policy_head.pol_payment,
policy_head.opt_64vb, policy_address.ph_no,
policy_address.email, policy_address.name_ac_holder,
policy_address.bank_ifsc_code,
policy_address.bank_ac_type,

policy_address.bank_address FROM policy_head,
   policy_address   WHERE (policy_head.ref_no =
policy_address.ref_no) and
   ((policy_head.ref_no = :no))
Dw_2.query:
 SELECT policy_det.ref_no,   policy_det.slno,
policy_det.ghpl_id,   policy_det.name_insured,
   policy_det.dob, policy_det.age,
policy_det.sex,   policy_det.occupation,
policy_det.relation,
   policy_det.sum_insured,
policy_det.bonus_amount,
   policy_det.bal_amount,
policy_det.remarks,   policy_det.usrcd,
policy_det.sysdate,   policy_det.cum_prc,
policy_det.sum_ins1,   policy_det.cum_prc1,
policy_det.bon_amt1,   policy_det.sum_ins2,
policy_det.cum_prc2,   policy_det.bon_amt2,
policy_det.dom_hosp,   policy_det.photo_path,
policy_det.photo_ys,   policy_det.finyear,
policy_det.end_date,   policy_det.premium,
policy_det.pol_type,   policy_det.membercode
   FROM policy_det   WHERE policy_det.ref_no = :no
                    ****
Window code for the above screen
forward
global type w_policy from w_masterno2
end type
end forward
shared variables
end variables
global type w_policy from w_masterno2
long backcolor = 134217747
end type
global w_policy w_policy
type variables
string policy_no,agentcd

```
int finyear
end variables
on w_policy.create
int iCurrent
call super::create
end on
on w_policy.destroy
call super::destroy
end on
event open;call super::open;finyear=0
fyok='Y'
end event
type pb_12 from w_masterno2`pb_12 within w_policy
integer width = 302
integer height = 96
end type
event                               pb_12::clicked;call
super::clicked;open(w_ghpl_ids)
end event
type pb_2 from w_masterno2`pb_2 within w_policy
integer x = 3355
integer y = 1820
integer width = 265
integer height = 112
integer taborder = 60
end type
type pb_1 from w_masterno2`pb_1 within w_policy
integer x = 3090
integer y = 1820
integer width = 265
integer height = 112
integer taborder = 50
end type
type uo_1 from w_masterno2`uo_1 within w_policy
end type
```

```
event   uo_1::savebefore;call   super::savebefore;string
path,insured_name,add1,add2,add3,city,pincode,bank_
name,bank_acno,bank_city,ins_branch,izone,ph_no
string  name_ac_holder,bank_ifsc_code,  bank_ac_type,
email,bank_address
if left(flag,1)<>"D" then
dwitemstatus st
string mess
int ret
st=dw_1.getitemstatus(1,"ph_no",primary!)
if st=datamodified! or st=newmodified! then
        mess="Your Mediclaim Policy been registered
with          us          and          your          ref.no.
"+dw_1.getitemstring(1,"ghpl_id")
        ph_no=dw_1.getitemstring(1,"ph_no")
        if len(ph_no)=12 then
                ret=gf_smsdata(ph_no,mess)
        end if
end if
        if left(flag,1)="M" then
ref_no=dw_1.getitemnumber(1,"ref_no")
 SELECT ins_co_branch.co_cd     INTO :ins_co
   FROM policy_head,         ins_co_branch
   WHERE        (        policy_head.ins_branch        =
ins_co_branch.co_br_code ) and  ref_no=:ref_no ;
end if
ins_branch=dw_1.getitemstring(1,"ins_branch")
 SELECT ins_co_branch.co_cd  INTO :ins_co
   FROM ins_co_branch
   WHERE ins_co_branch.co_br_code = :ins_branch   ;
Else
ref_no=dw_1.getitemnumber(1,"ref_no",delete!,true)
ghpl_id=dw_1.getitemstring(1,"ghpl_id",delete!,true)
ttype='POLICY ENTRY INDIVIDUAL -0'
ctr=gf_deletedata()
end if
if flag='A' then
```

```
            vouno=dw_1.getitemnumber(1,"ref_no")
            ctr=vouno
 SELECT  max(policy_head.ref_no   )          INTO :vouno
FROM policy_head  ;
if isnull(vouno) then vouno=0
                vouno=vouno+1
                dw_1.setitem(1,"ref_no",vouno)
                dw_1.setitem(1,"finyear",finyear)
                     for ctr=1 to dw_2.rowcount()
            dw_2.setitem(ts,"ref_no",vouno)
next
//if ctr<>vouno then
ghpl_id=                              'GHPL-'+ins_co+'-
'+RightA('00000'+string(vouno),5)
            dw_1.setitem(1,"ghpl_id",ghpl_id)
            for ts=1 to dw_2.rowcount()
ghpl_id='GHPL-'+ins_co+'-
'+RightA('00000'+string(vouno),5)+'-'+string(ts)
            dw_2.setitem(ts,"ghpl_id",ghpl_id)
            dw_2.setitem(ts,"ref_no",vouno)
            dw_2.setitem(ts,"finyear",finyear)
next
gf_messask("Press Enter to Update",1)
//             end if
            vouno=dw_1.getitemnumber(1,"ref_no")
insured_name=dw_1.getitemstring(1,"insured_name")
            add1=dw_1.getitemstring(1,"add1")
            add2=dw_1.getitemstring(1,"add2")
            add3=dw_1.getitemstring(1,"add3")
            city=dw_1.getitemstring(1,"city")
            pincode=dw_1.getitemstring(1,"pincode")
bank_name=dw_1.getitemstring(1,"bank_name")
            bank_city=dw_1.getitemstring(1,"bank_city")
            izone=dw_1.getitemstring(1,"izone")
            ph_no=dw_1.getitemstring(1,"ph_no")
name_ac_holder=dw_1.getitemstring(1,"name_ac_hold
er")
```

```
bank_ifsc_code=dw_1.getitemstring(1,"bank_ifsc_code
")
bank_ac_type=dw_1.getitemstring(1,"bank_ac_type")
email=dw_1.getitemstring(1,"email")
bank_address=dw_1.getitemstring(1,"bank_address")
SELECT count(*)    INTO :ctr    FROM policy_address
WHERE policy_address.ref_no = :vouno   ;
if ctr>0 then
  UPDATE policy_address
    SET insured_name = :insured_name,        add1 =
:add1,        add2 = :add2,   add3 = :add3,        city =
:city,          pincode = :pincode,    usrcd = :g_login,
sysdate = :sysdatetime,        ghpl_id = :ghpl_id,
bank_name = :bank_name,  bank_acno = :bank_acno,
bank_city = :bank_city  ,izone=:izone, fincode=:finyear,
ph_no=:ph_no,name_ac_holder=:name_ac_holder,
bank_ifsc_code=:bank_ifsc_code,bank_ac_type=:bank_
ac_type,        email=:email,
bank_address=:bank_address
  WHERE    policy_address.ref_no   =    :vouno   and
isnull(fincode,0)>=:finyear  ;
  UPDATE policy_address
    SET    usrcd = :g_login,        sysdate = :sysdatetime,
ghpl_id  =  :ghpl_id,  bank_name  =  :bank_name,
bank_acno  =  :bank_acno,bank_city  =  :bank_city    ,
izone=:izone,fincode=:finyear,ph_no=:ph_no
,name_ac_holder=:name_ac_holder,
bank_ifsc_code=:bank_ifsc_code,
bank_ac_type=:bank_ac_type, email=:email,
bank_address=:bank_address
  WHERE policy_address.ref_no = :vouno   ;
else
INSERT INTO policy_address
      ( ref_no,         insured_name,          add1,
add2,       add3,        city,        pincode,
```

```
        usrcd,              sysdate,                ghpl_id,
bank_name,                              bank_acno,
bank_city,izone,fincode,ph_no,name_ac_holder,
bank_ifsc_code,bank_ac_type,email,bank_address )
 VALUES ( :vouno,           :insured_name,       :add1,
:add2,       :add3,        :city,        :pincode,
        :g_login,           :sysdatetime,           :ghpl_id,
:bank_name,:bank_acno,:bank_city,:izone,0,:ph_no,:na
me_ac_holder,
:bank_ifsc_code,:bank_ac_type,:email,:bank_address   )
;
        end if
for ctr=1 to dw_2.rowcount()
ghpl_id=dw_2.getitemstring(ctr,"ghpl_id")
if ins_co="NIA" then
if                  ctr<10                  then
path="\\newserver\d\ghpl_img_nia\"+RightA(trim(
ghpl_id ),7)+".jpg"
else
        path="\\newserver\d\ghpl_img_nia\"+RightA(tr
im( ghpl_id ),8)+".jpg"
end if
elseif left(ins_co,1)="O" then
if ctr<10 then
path="\\newserver\d\ghpl_img_oih\"+RightA(trim(
ghpl_id ),7)+".jpg"
else
path="\\newserver\d\ghpl_img_oih\"+RightA(trim(
ghpl_id ),8)+".jpg"
end if
        elseif ins_co="UIH" or ins_co="UIA" then
if ctr<10 then
        path="\\newserver\d\ghpl_img_uim\"+RightA(t
rim( ghpl_id ),7)+".jpg"
                else
        path="\\newserver\d\ghpl_img_uim\"+RightA(t
rim( ghpl_id ),8)+".jpg"
```

```
                        end if
                elseif left(ins_co,2)="UI" THEN
                        if ctr<10 then
path="\\newserver\d\ghpl_img_uim\"+RightA(trim(
ghpl_id ),7)+".jpg"
                        else
path="\\newserver\d\ghpl_img_uim\"+RightA(trim(
ghpl_id ),8)+".jpg"
end if
                elseif left(ins_co,1)="N" THEN
                        if ctr<10 then
path="\\newserver\d\ghpl_img_nat\"+RightA(trim(
ghpl_id ),7)+".jpg"
else
                path="\\newserver\d\ghpl_img_nat\"+RightA(t
rim( ghpl_id ),8)+".jpg"
                        end if
                elseif left(ins_co,1)="R" THEN
                        if ctr<10 then
                path="\\newserver\d\ghpl_img_rgi\"+RightA(tri
m( ghpl_id ),7)+".jpg"
                        else
                path="\\newserver\d\ghpl_img_rgi\"+RightA(tri
m( ghpl_id ),8)+".jpg"
                        end if
                END IF
                        dw_2.setitem(ctr,"photo_path",path)
                next
                elseif LeftA(flag,1)='M' then
                vouno=dw_1.getitemnumber(1,"ref_no")
insured_name=dw_1.getitemstring(1,"insured_name")
                add1=dw_1.getitemstring(1,"add1")
add2=dw_1.getitemstring(1,"add2")
add3=dw_1.getitemstring(1,"add3")
city=dw_1.getitemstring(1,"city")
pincode=dw_1.getitemstring(1,"pincode")
bank_name=dw_1.getitemstring(1,"bank_name")
```

```
                bank_acno=dw_1.getitemstring(1,"bank_acno")
                bank_city=dw_1.getitemstring(1,"bank_city")
                izone=dw_1.getitemstring(1,"izone")
                ph_no=dw_1.getitemstring(1,"ph_no")
        name_ac_holder=dw_1.getitemstring(1,"name_ac_hold
        er")
        bank_ifsc_code=dw_1.getitemstring(1,"bank_ifsc_code
        ")
        bank_ac_type=dw_1.getitemstring(1,"bank_ac_type")
        email=dw_1.getitemstring(1,"email")
        bank_address=dw_1.getitemstring(1,"bank_address")
        UPDATE policy_address
           SET insured_name = :insured_name,          add1 =
        :add1,        add2 = :add2,
              add3 = :add3,          city = :city,          pincode =
        :pincode,
              usrcd = :g_login,          sysdate = :sysdatetime,
        ghpl_id = :ghpl_id,
              bank_name = :bank_name,               bank_acno =
        :bank_acno,          bank_city          =          :bank_city
        ,izone=:izone,ph_no=:ph_no,
        name_ac_holder=:name_ac_holder,
        bank_ifsc_code=:bank_ifsc_code,
        bank_ac_type=:bank_ac_type,
        email=:email, bank_address=:bank_address
         WHERE      policy_address.ref_no      =      :vouno      and
        fincode>=:finyear ;
        end if
        if LeftA(flag,1)='M' then
                        for ctr=1 to dw_2.rowcount()
                dw_2.setitem(ctr,"ref_no",vouno)
                ghpl_id=dw_2.getitemstring(ctr,"ghpl_id")
                                if ins_co="NIA" then
                                if ctr<10 then
        path="\\newserver\d\ghpl_img_nia\"+RightA(trim(
        ghpl_id ),7)+".jpg"
                        else
```

```
                path="\\newserver\d\ghpl_img_nia\"+RightA(tr
im( ghpl_id ),8)+".jpg"
                end if
        ELSEif    ins_co="UIH"    or    ins_co='UIC'    OR
ins_co='UIA' then
                        if ctr<10 then
        path="\\newserver\d\ghpl_img_uih\"+RightA(tr
im( ghpl_id ),7)+".jpg"
                else
        path="\\newserver\d\ghpl_img_uih\"+RightA(tr
im( ghpl_id ),8)+".jpg"
                end if
        elseif left(ins_co,1)="O" then
                        if ctr<10 then
        path="\\newserver\d\ghpl_img_oih\"+RightA(tr
im( ghpl_id ),7)+".jpg"
                else
        path="\\newserver\d\ghpl_img_oih\"+RightA(tr
im( ghpl_id ),8)+".jpg"
                end if
        ELSEif ins_co="UIM" then
                if ctr<10 then
        path="\\newserver\d\ghpl_img_uim\"+RightA(t
rim( ghpl_id ),7)+".jpg"
                else
        path="\\newserver\d\ghpl_img_uim\"+RightA(t
rim( ghpl_id ),8)+".jpg"
                end if
        elseif left(ins_co,1)="N" THEN
                        if ctr<10 then
        path="\\newserver\d\ghpl_img_nat\"+RightA(t
rim( ghpl_id ),7)+".jpg"
                else
        path="\\newserver\d\ghpl_img_nat\"+RightA(t
rim( ghpl_id ),8)+".jpg"
                end if
end if
```

```
     dw_2.getitemstatus(ctr,0,primary!)=newmodified! then
          dw_2.setitem(ctr,"photo_path",path)
     end if
          string p_path
          p_path=dw_2.getitemstring(ctr,"photo_path")
          if isnull(p_path) then p_path=""
          if p_path='' then
          dw_2.setitem(ctr,"photo_path",path)
          end if
     next
     policy_no=dw_1.getitemstring(1,"policy_no")
     agentcd=dw_1.getitemstring(1,"agentcd")
     end if
     end event
     event                                    uo_1::cancel;call
     super::cancel;dw_1.settaborder("ghpl_id",0)
          SELECT max(policy_head.ref_no  )
       INTO :vouno
       FROM policy_head  ;
     if isnull(vouno) then vouno=0
          vouno=vouno+1
     dw_1.setitem(1,"ref_no",vouno)
     ghpl_id='GHPL-'+ins_co+'-'+RightA('00000'+
     string(vouno),5)
     dw_1.setitem(1,"ghpl_id",ghpl_id)
     if         not         isnull(policy_no)         then
     dw_1.setitem(1,"policy_no",LeftA(policy_no,12))
     if         not         isnull(agentcd)           then
     dw_1.setitem(1,"agentcd",agentcd)
          dw_1.getchild("policy_no",dwc)
          dwc.settransobject(sqlca)
          dwc.setfilter("")
          dwc.filter()
     end event
     event                                    uo_1::modify;call
     super::modify;dw_1.settaborder("ghpl_id",150)
     end event
```

```
event    uo_1::saveafter;call    super::saveafter;string
membercode,ph_no,mess
int ret
if ins_co='NIA' then
for ctr=1 to dw_2.rowcount()
        ghpl_id=dw_2.getitemstring(ctr,"ghpl_id")
membercode=dw_2.getitemstring(ctr,"membercode")
        if    not    isnull(membercode)    and
trim(membercode)<>" then
  UPDATE policy_det_ren    S
ET membercode = :membercode
WHERE policy_det_ren.ghpl_id = :ghpl_id   ;
end if
next
end if
end event
type  pb_name  from  w_masterno2`pb_name  within
w_policy
integer x = 2149
integer width = 727
integer height = 152
string text = "Policy Entry"
end type
type mle_1 from w_masterno2`mle_1 within w_policy
integer height = 156
boolean originalsize = false
end type
type dw_2 from w_masterno2`dw_2 within w_policy
integer x = 64
integer y = 1120
integer width = 3511
integer height = 744
integer taborder = 40
string dataobject = "d_policy_det"
end type
```

```
event                        dw_2::itemchanged;call
super::itemchanged;er_flag   =    super::    event
itemchanged(row,dwo,data)
choose case er_flag
        case 0
        case else
                return 1
end choose
date dt
int age
choose case dwo.name
        case "name_insured"
f dw_2.rowcount()=row then
dw_2.insertrow(0)
dw_2.setitem(row,"slno",row)
dw_2.setitem(row,"ghpl_id",trim(dw_1.getitemstring(1,
"ghpl_id"))+'-'+string(row))
        CASE "sum_insured"
        dw_2.setitem(row,"bal_amount",real(data))
        case "cum_prc"
        dw_2.setitem(row,"bonus_amount",dw_2.getit
emnumber(row,"sum_insured")*real(data)/100)
        case "cum_prc1"
dw_2.setitem(row,"bon_amt1",dw_2.getitemnumber(r
ow,"sum_ins1")*real(data)/100)
        case "cum_prc2"
        dw_2.setitem(row,"bon_amt2",dw_2.getitemn
umber(row,"sum_ins2")*real(data)/100)
        case "occupation"
                dw_1.getchild('occupation',dwc)
                dwc.settransobject(sqlca)
occupation=dwc.getitemstring(dwc.getrow(),
"occupation")
        case "relation"
        CASE "dob"
                dt=date(left(data,10))
        if dt>date('1900/01/01') then
```

```
                    age=year(today())-year(dt)
                    dw_2.setitem(row,"age",age)
            end if
            case "sex"
            if data="M" then
                    elseif data='F' then
                    else
                    gf_messask("Wrong Sex",1)
                    er_flag=1
                    return 1
            end if
end choose
IF ins_co="NIA" or left(ins_co,1)="U" THEN
 else
choose case dwo.name
        CASE "bonus_amount"
                amt=real(data)
                dw_2.setitem(row,"cum_prc",amt/dw_2.getite
mnumber(row, "sum_insured")*100)
        case "bon_amt1"
                amt=real(data)
                dw_2.setitem(row,"cum_prc1",amt/dw_2.getit
emnumber(row, "sum_ins1")*100)
        case "bon_amt2"
                amt=real(data)
                dw_2.setitem(row,"cum_prc2",amt/dw_2.getit
emnumber(row, "sum_ins2")*100)
end choose
end if
end event
type dw_1 from w_masterno2`dw_1 within w_policy
integer x = 261
integer y = 176
integer width = 3118
integer height = 872
integer taborder = 30
string dataobject = "d_policy_head"
```

```
end type
event                                        dw_1::itemchanged;call
super::itemchanged;er_flag      =      super::      event
itemchanged(row,dwo,data)
choose case er_flag
        case 0
        case else
        return 1
end choose
string
remark1,remark2,remark3,remark4,cd,co_reg_cd,co_br
_code
date dt,dt1,policy_from,policy_to
string ghpl_id1
long sno
if dwo.name="ref_no" then
policy_from=date(dw_1.getitemdatetime(row,"policy_f
rom"))
        policy_to=date(dw_1.getitemdatetime(row,"pol
icy_to"))
                        ref_no=real(data)
ghpl_id=dw_1.getitemstring(row,"ghpl_id")+"%"
  SELECT ins_co_branch.co_cd    INTO :ins_co
    FROM policy_head,        ins_co_branch
    WHERE        (        policy_head.ins_branch        =
ins_co_branch.co_br_code ) and  ref_no=:ref_no ;
  SELECT count(*)    INTO :ctr
    FROM pre_approvals
    WHERE ( pre_approvals.ghpl_id like :ghpl_id ) AND
    ( pre_approvals.adm_date between :policy_from and
:policy_to ) ;
gf_messask(string(ctr),1)
        if ctr>0 then
                if g_login<>"00" then
gf_messask("Pre-Authorisation    Raised    -    Can    not
Modify",1)
        dw_2.Object.DataWindow.ReadOnly="Yes"
```

```
                dw_1.Object.DataWindow.ReadOnly="Yes"
                else
gf_messask("Pre-Authorisation   Raised   -   Should   not
Modify",1)
                end if
        end if
end if
choose case flag
        case "MG"
                if dwo.name="policy_from" then
                        policy_from=date(left(data,10))
                policy_to=date(dw_1.getitemdatetime(row,"pol
icy_to"))
if daysafter(policy_from,policy_to)>366 then
gf_messask("Cannot Change Date Range",1)
        return 1
end if
elseif dwo.name="policy_to" then
policy_to=date(left(data,10))
policy_from=date(dw_1.getitemdatetime(row,"policy_f
rom"))
if daysafter(policy_from,policy_to)>366 then
gf_messask("Cannot Change Date Range",1)
return 1
end if
end if
case "VG"
CASE "DG"
dt=date(dw_1.getitemdatetime(1,"policy_from"))
dt1=date(dw_1.getitemdatetime(1,"policy_to"))
ghpl_id=dw_1.getitemstring(1,"ghpl_id")+'%'
  SELECT count(claims.cl_no  )   INTO :ctr
   FROM claims,        pre_approvals
   WHFRE       (        pre_approvals.pre_app_no       =
claims.pre_app_no ) and
      ( ( claims.adm_date between :dt and :dt1 ) AND
      ( pre_approvals.ghpl_id like :ghpl_id ) )   ;
```

```
if ctr>0 then
gf_messask("This Policy Contains Claims - Cannot be
deleted",1)
uo_1.pb_save.enabled=false
end if
case "A"
if dwo.name='policy_no' then
if LenA(data)<6 then
gf_messask("Please enter valid Policy No",1)
        return 1
end if
 SELECT count(*)    INTO :ctr
 FROM policy_head    WHERE policy_head.policy_no =
:data  ;
        if ctr>0 then
                gf_messask("This Policy No is already
entered",1)
                return 1
        end if
 SELECT count(*)    INTO :ctr
  FROM policy_head_ren    WHERE policy_no = :data  ;
        if ctr>0 then
gf_messask("This Policy No is already entered in
Renewal",1)
return 1
end if
cd=LeftA(data,6)+"%"
 SELECT ins_co_branch.co_reg_cd,
     ins_co_branch.co_br_code ,ins_co_branch.co_cd
  INTO :co_reg_cd,
     :co_br_code ,:ins_co
  FROM ins_co_branch
 WHERE ins_co_branch.co_ins_cd like :cd  ;
        if sqlca.sqlcode=100 then
        gf_messask("Branch Code Not Found ",1)
        return 1
        end if
```

```
            dw_1.setitem(1,"ins_reg",co_reg_cd)
            dw_1.setitem(1,"ins_co",ins_co)
            dw_1.setitem(1,"ins_branch",co_br_code)
            if not isnulL(co_br_code) then
dw_1.setitem(1,"ins_co",ins_co)
ghpl_id1='GHPL-'+ins_co+'%'
sno=dw_1.getitemnumber(1,"ref_no")
ghpl_id='GHPL-'+ins_co+'-'+right('00000'+string(sno),5)
dw_1.setitem(1,"ghpl_id",ghpl_id)
ghpl_id=dw_1.getitemstring(row,"ghpl_id")
dw_2.setitem(1,"ghpl_id",ghpl_id+'-1')
dw_2.setitem(1,"slno",1)
if dw_2.rowcount()=1 then
dw_2.insertrow(0)
end if
                    if dwo.name='ins_co' then
                    ins_co=data
                    ghpl_id1='GHPL-'+ins_co+'%'
                    SELECT
max(convert(float,substring(policy_det.ghpl_id,10,5))  )
  INTO :sno
  FROM policy_det
  WHERE policy_det.ghpl_id like :ghpl_id1   ;
            if isnull(sno) then sno=0
                    sno=sno+1
                    ghpl_id='GHPL-'+ins_co+'-
'+RightA('00000'+string(sno),5)
                    dw_1.setitem(1,"ghpl_id",ghpl_id)
                    dw_2.setitem(1,"ghpl_id",ghpl_id+'-1')
                    dw_2.setitem(1,"slno",1)
                    if        dw_2.rowcount()=1        then
dw_2.insertrow(0)
            elseif dwo.name="insured_name" then
                    gf_messask(data,1)
                    dw_2.setitem(1,"name_insured",data)
end if
end if
```

```
end choose
choose case dwo.name
        case "co_cd"
                dw_1.getchild("co_reg_cd",dwc)
                dwc.settransobject(sqlca)
                dwc.setfilter("co_cd='"+data+"'")
                dwc.filter()
        case "policy_from"
                dt=date(LeftA(data,10))
                        if dt>today() then
                                gf_messask("Policy
From Date greater than Today",1)
                        end if
                dt1=gf_getnextyear(dt)
                dw_1.setitem(row,"policy_to",dt1)
                if dt<date('2004/06/01') then
                        gf_messask("Please  Check  the
date",1)
                        return 1
                end if
        case "net_premium"
                amt=real(data)
                amt=round(amt*0.1236,0)
                dw_1.setitem(row,"service_tax",amt)
        case "prev_policy_no"
SELECT count(*)   INTO :ctr
  FROM policy_head
  WHERE policy_head.policy_no = :data  ;
if ctr>0 then
 SELECT policy_head.ref_no    INTO :ctr
  FROM policy_head
  WHERE policy_head.policy_no = :data  ;
        gf_messask("This  Prev.Policy  is  entered  in
"+string(ctr)+" Please use Renewal",1)
elseif LeftA(data,4)='2004' or LeftA(data,4)='2005' then
gf_messask("Please enter policy no in format",1)
end if
```

```
end choose
if dwo.name="insured_name" then
 dw_2.setitem(1,"name_insured",data)
end if
end event
event   dw_1::editchanged;call   super::editchanged;if
dwo.name='ref_no' then
        if data<='9' then
                dw_1.getchild("ref_no",dwc)
                dwc.settransobject(sqlca)
dwc.setfilter("policy_no like '%"+UPPER(data)+"%'")
                dwc.filter()
        ELSEIF trim(data)="" then
                dw_1.getchild("ref_no",dwc)
                dwc.settransobject(sqlca)
                dwc.setfilter("")
                dwc.filter()
        else
                dw_1.getchild("ref_no",dwc)
                dwc.settransobject(sqlca)
dwc.setfilter("insured_name like'%"+UPPER(data)+"%'")
                dwc.filter()
                end if
end if
end event
type
sle_1 from w_masterno2`sle_1 within w_policy
end type
type rr_1 from w_masterno2`rr_1 within w_policy
integer x = 206
integer y = 160
integer width = 3227
integer height = 904
end type
type rr_2 from w_masterno2`rr_2 within w_policy
integer x = 32
integer y = 1084
```

integer width = 3575
integer height = 816
end type

****

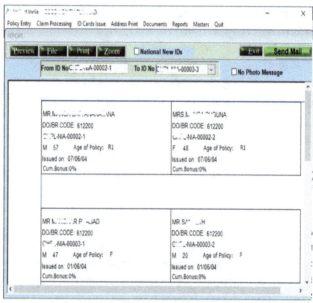

The query for dw_1: for the report

SELECT policy_head.policy_no,   policy_det.ghpl_id,
policy_det.name_insured,   policy_det.age,
policy_det.sex,   policy_head.policy_from,
policy_head.policy_to,   policy_det.photo_path,
pol_types.id_type,   policy_head.ins_co,
policy_head.decl_date,   BON=isnull(cum_prc,0)
FROM policy_head,pol_types,   policy_det
  WHERE (policy_head.pol_type = pol_types.pol_type)
and (policy_det.ref_no = policy_head.ref_no) and
      ((policy_det.ghpl_id between :frno and :tono))
The above is an id printing screen. Photos are not
printed on the above screen. These reports are set to
pre-printed labels.
Now the Ids are printed from the above screen, cut,
laminated, and dispatched.

An individual wants to join a hospital, he goes to the hospital shows his id and he is admitted and his details are sent to the TPA. The TPA received the data and verifies the data if he is eligible for the treatment and approval will be sent to the hospital else a denial will be sent to the hospital. For creating the approval, we need to enter the hospital request.

Once we receive the request a request entry will be made in the system. The details will include the id of the person, hospital name, name of the disease, and amount requested by the hospital for treatment. There will be a panel of doctors with the TPA who verifies the details of the disease and procedures and the expected amount and amount available in the individual policy and issue approval. Which is fed in the system and an approval letter is printed and sent to the hospital. If the request is denied a denial letter is printed and sent to the hospital.

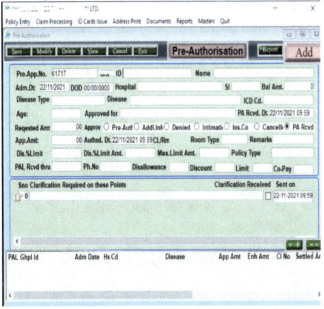

The query for dw_1:

```
SELECT                    pre_approvals.pre_app_no        ,
pre_approvals.ghpl_id ,         pre_approvals.adm_date ,
pre_approvals.hs_cd ,           pre_approvals.disease ,
pre_approvals.deptcode ,        pre_approvals.req_amt
,                       pre_approvals.app_amt   ,
pre_approvals.remarks ,         pre_approvals.usrcd ,
pre_approvals.sysdate ,         pre_approvals.flag ,
bal=0,          sum=0,          pre_approvals.app_date ,
pre_approvals.room_type                         ,
pre_approvals.nol_code,pre_approvals.intimation_date
, pre_approvals.loss_date ,pre_approvals.proc_desc ,
pre_approvals.doc_name ,pre_approvals.doc_address ,
pre_approvals.doc_qualification,pre_approvals.doc_reg
_no         ,       pre_approvals.doc_tel_no            ,
pre_approvals.age ,                  name=space(100),
prc_limit=0,        prc_amt=0,           max_limit=0,
pol_type='IND',         pre_approvals.disease_lim ,
pre_approvals.disease_sub                       ,
pre_approvals.pa_mode                           ,
pre_approvals.phone_no,         pre_approvals.email  ,
pre_approvals.disal_amt ,       pre_approvals.disc_amt ,
pre_approvals.limit_amt ,       pre_approvals.co_pay ,
pre_approvals.pre_cl_no                         FROM
pre_approvals
WHERE ( pre_approvals.pre_app_no = :no )
Second dw_2 query:
 SELECT pre_app_points.sno,  pre_app_points.points,
pre_app_points.pre_app_no, pre_app_points.usrcd,
pre_app_points.sysdate,  pre_app_points.flag,
pre_app_points.a_type,  pre_app_points.srno
   FROM pre_app_points
  WHERE ( pre_app_points.pre_app_no = :no ) AND
     ( pre_app_points.srno = 0 )
Third dw_3 query:
 SELECT DISTINCT v_pre_app_enh.pre_app_no,
v_pre_app_enh.ghpl_id,  v_pre_app_enh.adm_date,
v_pre_app_enh.hs_cd, v_pre_app_enh.disease,
```

v_pre_app_enh.app_amt, v_pre_app_enh.enh_amt,
v_pre_app_enh.cl_no, l_amt=v_pre_app_enh.set_amt,
v_pre_app_enh.chq_no, v_pre_app_enh.chq_dt,
v_pre_app_enh.status,v_pre_app_enh.doc_qualificatio
n,   v_pre_app_enh.dis_amt,claim=
v_pre_app_enh.cl_amt, v_pre_app_enh.flag
   FROM v_pre_app_enh
   WHERE v_pre_app_enh.ghpl_id like :cd

Sometimes an excess amount is requested from the
hospital, the same process is followed for the excess
amount, it is called enhancement of approval. At the
bottom of the screen is previous pre-authorizations.
These tables were used in pre-authorization of
hospitalization

```
TABLE [dbo].[pre_approvals](
        [pre_app_no] [int] NOT NULL,
        [ghpl_id] [varchar](25) NOT NULL,
        [adm_date] [datetime] NULL,
        [hs_cd] [varchar](5) NOT NULL,
        [disease] [varchar](100) NOT NULL,
        [deptcode] [varchar](6) NULL,
        [req_amt] [float] NOT NULL,
        [app_amt] [float] NOT NULL,
        [remarks] [varchar](200) NULL,
        [usrcd] [varchar](5) NULL,
        [sysdate] [datetime] NULL,
        [flag] [char](1) NULL,
        [app_date] [smalldatetime] NULL,
        [room_type] [varchar](20) NULL,
        [nol_code] [numeric](4, 0) NULL,
        [intimation_date] [smalldatetime] NULL,
        [loss_date] [smalldatetime] NULL,
        [proc_desc] [varchar](100) NULL,
        [doc_name] [varchar](50) NULL,
        [doc_address] [varchar](255) NULL,
        [doc_qualification] [varchar](25) NULL,
        [doc_reg_no] [varchar](50) NULL,
        [doc_tel_no] [varchar](50) NULL,
        [age] [int] NULL,
        [disease_lim] [varchar](20) NULL,
        [disease_sub] [varchar](8) NULL,
```

```
[pa_mode] [varchar](8) NULL,
[phone_no] [varchar](30) NULL,
[email] [varchar](30) NULL,
[disal_amt] [numeric](10, 0) NULL,
[disc_amt] [numeric](10, 0) NULL,
[limit_amt] [numeric](10, 0) NULL,
[co_pay] [numeric](10, 0) NULL,
[pre_cl_no] [numeric](7, 0) NULL,
```

TABLE [dbo].[pre_app_points](--- points given
by the hospitals are stored here
```
    [pre_app_no] [int] NOT NULL,
    [sno] [tinyint] NOT NULL,
    [points] [varchar](1200) NOT NULL,
    [usrcd] [varchar](5) NOT NULL,
    [sysdate] [datetime] NOT NULL,
    [flag] [char](1) NOT NULL,
    [a_type] [char](1) NULL,
    [srno] [tinyint] NULL,
```

[dbo].[pre_app_enhance](--enhancement of
hospitalisation amount.
```
    [pre_app_no] [int] NOT NULL,
    [sno] [tinyint] NOT NULL,
    [enh_date] [datetime] NOT NULL,
    [enh_req_amt] [float] NOT NULL,
    [enh_app_amt] [float] NOT NULL,
    [rem] [varchar](500) NULL,
    [usrcd] [varchar](5) NOT NULL,
    [sysdate] [datetime] NOT NULL,
```

First dw_1 query
  SELECT DISTINCT pre_approvals.pre_app_no,
pre_approvals.ghpl_id,   pre_approvals.adm_date,
pre_approvals.hs_cd,   pre_approvals.disease,
pre_approvals.deptcode,   pre_approvals.req_amt,
pre_approvals.app_amt,   pre_approvals.remarks,
pre_approvals.usrcd,   pre_approvals.sysdate,
pre_approvals.flag,   pre_approvals.app_date,
bal=0.00,   pre_approvals.room_type,
pre_approvals.nol_code,
pre_approvals.intimation_date,
pre_approvals.loss_date,   pre_approvals.proc_desc,
pre_approvals.doc_name,   pre_approvals.doc_address,
pre_approvals.doc_qualification,
pre_approvals.doc_reg_no,   pre_approvals.doc_tel_no,
pre_approvals.age,   pre_approvals.disease_lim,
prc_amt=0.00,   prc_limit=0.00,   max_limit=0.00,
sum=0.00   FROM pre_approvals
  WHERE pre_approvals.pre_app_no = :no

```
Dw_2.query:
 SELECT                          pre_app_enhance.sno,
pre_app_enhance.enh_date,
pre_app_enhance.enh_req_amt,
pre_app_enhance.enh_app_amt,
pre_app_enhance.rem,  pre_app_enhance.usrcd,
pre_app_enhance.pre_app_no,
pre_app_enhance.sysdate
   FROM pre_app_enhance
   WHERE pre_app_enhance.pre_app_no = :no
Dw_3 query:
 SELECT pre_app_points.sno,
pre_app_points.points,
pre_app_points.pre_app_no,
pre_app_points.usrcd,
pre_app_points.sysdate,
pre_app_points.flag,
pre_app_points.a_type,
pre_app_points.srno
   FROM pre_app_points
   WHERE ( pre_app_points.pre_app_no = :no ) AND
     ( pre_app_points.srno = :sno )
Dw_4 query:
 SELECT DISTINCT v_pre_app_enh.pre_app_no,
v_pre_app_enh.ghpl_id,  v_pre_app_enh.adm_date,
v_pre_app_enh.hs_cd,  v_pre_app_enh.disease,
v_pre_app_enh.app_amt,  v_pre_app_enh.enh_amt,
v_pre_app_enh.cl_no,  l_amt=v_pre_app_enh.set_amt,
v_pre_app_enh.chq_no,  v_pre_app_enh.chq_dt,
v_pre_app_enh.status,v_pre_app_enh.doc_qualificatio
n,                    v_pre_app_enh.dis_amt,claim=
v_pre_app_enh.cl_amt,  v_pre_app_enh.flag
   FROM v_pre_app_enh
   WHERE v_pre_app_enh.ghpl_id like :cd
```

Next, when the patient is discharged the hospital sends a claim with the documents to the TPA. If the patient pays for the treatment he can also submit the claim to the TPA with the supporting documents.

This claim receipt is entered in the system.

The following are the tables used in the claim process

```sql
TABLE dbo.claims(
        cl_no numeric(10, 0) NOT NULL,
        cl_date smalldatetime NOT NULL,
        pre_app_no int NOT NULL,
        cl_amt float NOT NULL,
        dis_amt float NOT NULL,
        settled_amt float NOT NULL,
        reason varchar(150) NOT NULL,
        remarks varchar(150) NOT NULL,
        usrcd varchar(5) NOT NULL,
        sysdate smalldatetime NOT NULL,
        ip_no varchar(10) NULL,
        dt_discharge smalldatetime NULL,
        pre_hosp float NULL,
        post_hosp float NULL,
        disease varchar(8) NULL,
        adm_date smalldatetime NULL,
        bill_no varchar(20) NULL,
        pre varchar(1) NULL,
        post varchar(1) NULL,
        bill varchar(1) NULL,
        app_amt float NULL,
        disc_amt float NULL,
        disease_desc varchar(100) NULL,
        flag char(1) NULL,
        status char(1) NULL,
        treatment varchar(200) NULL,
        disease1 varchar(8) NULL,
        clr_date smalldatetime NULL,
        clr_rdate smalldatetime NULL,
        proc_date smalldatetime NULL,
        room_days tinyint NULL,
        iccu_days tinyint NULL,
        pre_days tinyint NULL,
        post_days tinyint NULL,
        tr_doctor varchar(20) NULL,
        disease_sub varchar(20) NULL,
        pre_amt numeric(10, 0) NULL,
```

```sql
post_amt numeric(10, 0) NULL,
pre_frdt smalldatetime NULL,
pre_todt smalldatetime NULL,
post_frdt smalldatetime NULL,
post_todt smalldatetime NULL,
pre_cl numeric(10, 0) NULL,
post_cl numeric(10, 0) NULL,
no_days int NULL,
proc_code varchar(50) NULL,
tds_amt numeric(10, 0) NULL,
room_cl numeric(10, 0) NULL,
room_pd numeric(10, 0) NULL,
icc_cl numeric(10, 0) NULL,
iccu_pd numeric(10, 0) NULL,
doc_fees_cl numeric(10, 0) NULL,
doc_fees_pd numeric(10, 0) NULL,
reg_fees_cl numeric(10, 0) NULL,
reg_fees_pd numeric(10, 0) NULL,
lab_cl numeric(10, 0) NULL,
lab_pd numeric(10, 0) NULL,
food_cl numeric(10, 0) NULL,
food_pd numeric(10, 0) NULL,
ot_cl numeric(10, 0) NULL,
ot_pd numeric(10, 0) NULL,
med_cl numeric(10, 0) NULL,
med_pd numeric(10, 0) NULL,
nur_chg_cl numeric(10, 0) NULL,
nur_chg_pd numeric(10, 0) NULL,
oth_cl numeric(10, 0) NULL,
oth_pd numeric(10, 0) NULL,
bill_amt numeric(10, 0) NULL,
det_rem varchar(255) NULL,
hosp_conf_amt numeric(10, 0) NULL,
amb_cl numeric(10, 0) NULL,
amb_pd numeric(10, 0) NULL,
tds_arr numeric(10, 0) NOT NULL,
co_pmt numeric(10, 0) NULL,
br_user varchar(10) NULL,
serv_tax numeric(9, 0) NULL,
serv_tax_org numeric(10, 2) NULL,
pr_cause varchar(10) NULL,
sec_cause varchar(10) NULL,
dt_symptoms datetime NULL,
pr_code1 varchar(10) NULL,
pr_code2 varchar(10) NULL,
```

```
        pr_code3 varchar(10) NULL,
        med_history1 varchar(240) NULL,
        med_history2 varchar(240) NULL,
        med_history3 varchar(240) NULL,
        diag2 varchar(10) NULL,
        diag3 varchar(10) NULL,
        bodypart varchar(10) NULL,
        diagnosic varchar(100) NULL,
        surgery_type varchar(20) NULL,
        excl_1 varchar(1) NULL,
        excl_2 varchar(1) NULL,
        excl_3 varchar(1) NULL,
        pre_ex_1 varchar(200) NULL,
        pre_ex_2 varchar(200) NULL,
        pre_ex_3 varchar(200) NULL,
        med_hist_1 varchar(200) NULL,
        med_hist_2 varchar(200) NULL,
        med_hist_3 varchar(200) NULL,
        name_ill_opr varchar(200) NULL,
        room_nurs_chg numeric(10, 0) NULL,
        surgery_chq numeric(10, 0) NULL,
        consult_chg numeric(10, 0) NULL,
        diag_chg numeric(10, 0) NULL,
        med_chg numeric(10, 0) NULL,
        misc_chg numeric(10, 0) NULL,
        upload varchar(1) NULL)
TABLE [dbo].[claim_chklist](
        [cl_no] [int] NOT NULL,
        [sno] [int] NOT NULL,
        [chk_cd] [varchar](5) NOT NULL,
        [yesno] [char](1) NOT NULL,
        [rems] [varchar](30) NOT NULL,
        [usrcd] [varchar](5) NOT NULL,
        [sysdate] [smalldatetime] NOT NULL,

TABLE [dbo].[claim_items](
        [cl_no] [numeric](10, 0) NOT NULL,
        [sno] [tinyint] NOT NULL,
        [cl_item] [varchar](5) NOT NULL,
        [cl_item_amt] [float] NOT NULL,
        [cl_dis_app_amt] [float] NULL,
        [cl_app_amt] [float] NULL,
        [rem] [varchar](100) NOT NULL,
        [usrcd] [varchar](5) NOT NULL,
        [sysdate] [smalldatetime] NOT NULL,
```

```
                    [srno] [tinyint] NULL,
        TABLE [dbo].[claim_points](
                    [claim_no] [numeric](10, 0) NOT NULL,
                    [sno] [tinyint] NOT NULL,
                    [points] [varchar](900) NOT NULL,
                    [flag] [char](1) NULL,
                    [usrcd] [varchar](5) NOT NULL,
                    [sysdate] [smalldatetime] NOT NULL,
                    [ins_flag] [char](1) NULL,
        TABLE [dbo].[claims_data](
                    [cl_no] [int] NOT NULL,
                    [cl_date] [smalldatetime] NOT NULL,
                    [pre_app_no] [int] NOT NULL,
                    [cl_amt] [float] NOT NULL,
                    [dis_amt] [float] NOT NULL,
                    [settled_amt] [float] NOT NULL,
                    [reason] [char](50) NOT NULL,
                    [remarks] [char](50) NOT NULL,
                    [usrcd] [char](5) NOT NULL,
                    [sysdate] [smalldatetime] NOT NULL,
                    [ip_no] [char](10) NULL,
                    [dt_discharge] [smalldatetime] NULL,
                    [pre_hosp] [float] NULL,
                    [post_hosp] [float] NULL,
                    [disease] [char](8) NULL,
                    [bill_no] [char](20) NULL,
                    [adm_date] [smalldatetime] NULL,
                    [ghpl_id] [char](25) NULL,
                    [hospital] [char](30) NULL,
                    [pre] [char](1) NULL,
                    [post] [char](1) NULL,
                    [bill] [char](1) NULL,
                    [app_amt] [float] NULL,
                    [disc_amt] [float] NULL,
                    [disease_desc] [char](20) NULL,
                    [flag] [char](1) NULL,
                    [room_nurs_chg] [numeric](10, 0) NULL,
                    [surgery_chq] [numeric](10, 0) NULL,
                    [consult_chg] [numeric](10, 0) NULL,
                    [diag_chg] [numeric](10, 0) NULL,
                    [med_chg] [numeric](10, 0) NULL,
                    [misc_chg] [numeric](10, 0) NULL,
                    [hosp_cd] [char](5) NULL,
                    [chq_dt] [smalldatetime] NULL
```

Dw_1.query:

```
SELECT claims.cl_no,          claims.cl_amt,
       claims.pre_app_no,         claims.dis_amt,
       claims.settled_amt,        claims.reason,
       claims.remarks,        claims.usrcd,
       claims.sysdate,        claims.ip_no,
       claims.dt_discharge,          claims.pre_hosp,
       claims.post_hosp,       claims.disease,
       claims.bill_no,         claims.adm_date,
       claims.pre,       claims.post,
       claims.bill,        claims.app_amt,
       claims.disc_amt,         claims.disease_desc,
       claims.flag,      claims.status,
       claims.clr_date,         claims.clr_rdate,
       claims.disease1,          claims.treatment,
       claims.cl_date,        claims.proc_date,
       claims.room_days,          claims.iccu_days,
       claims.pre_days,        claims.post_days,
       claims.tr_doctor,          claims.disease_sub,
       claims.pre_amt,        claims.post_amt,
```

```
    claims.pre_frdt,          claims.pre_todt,
    claims.post_frdt,         claims.post_todt,
    claims.pre_cl,          claims.post_cl,
    claims.no_days,           claims.bill_amt,
    claims.hosp_conf_amt,         claims.tds_arr,
    claims.co_pmt,          claims.br_user,
    claims.serv_tax,          claims.serv_tax_org,
    claims.tds_amt,          bano=space(10),
    badate=sysdate,          claims.upload
  FROM claims    WHERE claims.cl_no = :no
Dw_2 query:
  SELECT                claim_status.cl_no,
claim_status.bank_ac,  claim_status.bank_date,
claim_status.hosp_conf,  claim_status.hosp_date,
claim_status.def_doc_sent,  claim_status.def_doc_rec,
claim_status.def_doc_sent1,
claim_status.def_doc_rec1,
claim_status.med_scrutiny_rec,
claim_status.med_scrutiny_compl,
claim_status.for_rejection,  claim_status.sent_do_br,
claim_status.rec_do_br,  claim_status.sent_ro,
claim_status.rec_ro,  claim_status.sent_br,
claim_status.rec_br,  claim_status.final_reject,
claim_status.gen_scrutiny_rec,
laim_status.gen_scrutiny_done,
claim_status.gen_scrutiny_rem,
claim_status.pay_chq_no,  claim_status.pay_chq_dt,
claim_status.pay_cour_dt,  claim_status.pay_cour_no,
claim_status.pay_post_dt,    claim_status.chq_returns,
claim_status.chq_ret_remarks,  claim_status.sysdate,
claim_status.usrcd,  claim_status.rem1,
claim_status.rem2,  claim_status.def_rem1,
claim_status.def_rem2,  claim_status.def_rem3
 FROM claim_status
WHERE claim_status.cl_no = :cl_no
Dw_3 query:
```

```
SELECT    claim_points.sno,    claim_points.points,
claim_points.flag,  claim_points.usrcd,
claim_points.claim_no,  claim_points.sysdate,
claim_points.ins_flag    FROM claim_points
WHERE claim_points.claim_no = :NO
```

The claim is processed by the claims executive. Sometimes more details are required from the hospital. These details are fed into the system. If an individual claims the amount, then clarification is asked from the hospital. The request for more details if required is sent to the hospital and the claim status is set to under process. If the claim is payable each item from the bill is entered with the amount charges. For example, room rent is 10000, medicines are 5000. These items are entered. If the full amount is payable amount is entered as 10000, else only 9000 is payable it is entered as 9000, and 1000 is shown as declined. So, each amount is checked and the payable amount is entered. The final amount is treated as payable and declined amount. There are many processes are involved in the claim processing, which is entered through the claim registration and claim processing screens. Every process in the claim processing is documented through the screens.

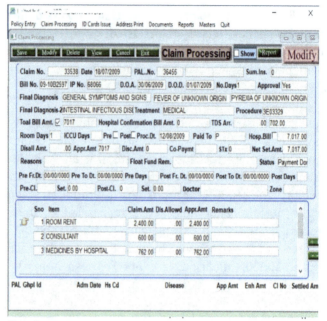

Dw_1 query:

A claim sheet is printed and for the final payable amount, a cheque is prepared and sent for signature. So, based on these processes screens are prepared and printout report screens are provided.

The following is the settlement letter screen:

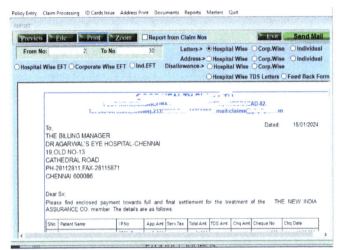

The report format in Pdf:

Query for this report:
SELECT pre_approvals.ghpl_id,   claims.ip_no,
    claims.settled_amt,   settlements.chq_no,
    settlements.set_amt,   hospitals.hs_name,
    hospitals.co_add1,   hospitals.co_add2,
    hospitals.co_add3,   hospitals.city,
    hospitals.pincode,   hospitals.hs_cd,
    settlements.chq_dt,   ins_com.co_name,

claims.br_user,   claims.serv_tax,
claims.tds_arr,   claims.tds_amt,
settlements.trans_id   FROM settlements,
hospitals,   claims,   pre_approvals,
ins_com   WHERE   (claims.pre_app_no   =
pre_approvals.pre_app_no) and
        (claims.cl_no = settlements.cl_no) and
        (settlements.paid_to = hospitals.hs_cd) and
        ((settlements.set_no between :frno and :tono))

Float fund statement:

FLOAT FUND REPLENISHMENT STATEMENT FOR THE PERIOD FROM 01-01-2011 TO 31-01-2011

Srl	GHPL ID	Policy No.	Insured Name	H.No.	D.O.A.	Bill Amt. Paid by Member	Bill Amt. Paid by Post	Pre. Post	Float Bill Allowed	Dis- allowed Amount	Ailment	Claims Settled Amt	Paid to Mem./ Proc.	Pymt Dt.
	Empno	Group Name	Beneficiary Name	Cl.No.	D.O.D.		GHPL	Hosp. Exp.	Amount	Amt	Reasons for Disallowance			GH/LNt
BRANCH/DO CODE	610100													
1														
2														
3														
				TOTALS										

Query for this:
SELECT   ins_co_branch.br_desc,
v_polivy_det.policy_no,
v_polivy_det.policy_from,
        v_polivy_det.policy_to,
v_polivy_det.insured_name,
v_polivy_det.name_insured,
v_polivy_det.ghpl_id,   v_polivy_det.age,
        v_polivy_det.sex,   v_polivy_det.relation,
        claims.cl_no,   claims.cl_date,
        claims.cl_amt,   claims.dt_discharge,
        hospitals.hs_name,   claims.disease_desc,
        claims.disease,   settlements.set_amt,
        settlements.chq_dt,   settlements.chq_no,
        claims.flag,   claims.pre_hosp,
        claims.post_hosp,   claims.settled_amt,
        claims.pre_app_no,   claims.dis_amt,
        claims.reason,   pre_approvals.hs_cd,
        settlements.pd_to,   claims.disc_amt,
        v_polivy_det.emp_no,   v_polivy_det.corp_cd,
        v_polivy_det.ins_branch,   claims.adm_date,

101

```
ins_co_branch.co_reg_cd,
ins_co_branch.co_br_code,
    ins_co_branch.co_cd,        corporates.corp_desc,
ins_co_branch.email_id,      v_polivy_det.pol_type,
v_polivy_det.sum_insured,   pre_approvals.app_date,
pre_amt=isnull(claims.pre_amt, 0),
post_amt=isnull(claims.post_amt, 0),            agentcd=
isnull(v_polivy_det.agentcd,corporates.agentcd),
dev_officer=isnull(v_polivy_det.dev_officer,corporates.
dev_officer),        pre_approvals.intimation_date,
v_polivy_det.disp_date, pre_cl=isnull(claims.pre_cl, 0),
post_cl=isnull( claims.post_cl, 0),
v_polivy_det.finyear,  v_polivy_det.izone,
claims.treatment,   pomcity.descript,
disases.disease_disc,  v_polivy_det.bonus,
claims.serv_tax,  claims.det_rem,
v_polivy_det.remarks,  v_polivy_det.pol_types,
claims.co_pmt,        claims.pre,
    claims.post,        claims.bill,
    claims.proc_code,        claims.disease_sub,
    claims.upload,        pre_approvals.adm_date
  FROM claims,        disases,        pre_approvals,
    settlements,        v_polivy_det,        hospitals,
    ins_co_branch,    corporates,        pomcity
  WHERE ( claims.disease *= disases.disease ) and
( v_polivy_det.ins_branch = ins_co_branch.co_br_code
)      and            (      claims.pre_app_no      =
pre_approvals.pre_app_no ) and
    ( claims.cl_no = settlements.cl_no ) and
( pre_approvals.ghpl_id = v_polivy_det.ghpl_id ) and
( claims.adm_date >= v_polivy_det.policy_from ) and
    ( claims.adm_date <= v_polivy_det.policy_to ) and
    ( pre_approvals.hs_cd = hospitals.hs_cd ) and
    ( v_polivy_det.corp_cd = corporates.corp_cd ) and
    ( hospitals.city = pomcity.citycd ) and
    ( ( settlements.chq_dt between :frdt and :todt ) )
```

The master menu for this application

Source for these menu which can be converted to Menu:

```
forward
global type w_mastermenu from window
end type
type dw_3 from datawindow within w_mastermenu
end type
type dw_1 from datawindow within w_mastermenu
end type
type tab_1 from tab within w_mastermenu
end type
type tabpage_1 from userobject within tab_1
end type
type pb_69 from picturebutton within tabpage_1
end type
type pb_63 from picturebutton within tabpage_1
end type
type pb_75 from picturebutton within tabpage_1
end type
type pb_74 from picturebutton within tabpage_1
end type
type pb_71 from picturebutton within tabpage_1
```

```
end type
type pb_68 from picturebutton within tabpage_1
end type
type pb_67 from picturebutton within tabpage_1
end type
type pb_66 from picturebutton within tabpage_1
end type
type pb_65 from picturebutton within tabpage_1
end type
type pb_64 from picturebutton within tabpage_1
end type
type pb_62 from picturebutton within tabpage_1
end type
type pb_61 from picturebutton within tabpage_1
end type
type pb_60 from picturebutton within tabpage_1
end type
type pb_57 from picturebutton within tabpage_1
end type
type pb_56 from picturebutton within tabpage_1
end type
type pb_55 from picturebutton within tabpage_1
end type
type pb_54 from picturebutton within tabpage_1
end type
type pb_53 from picturebutton within tabpage_1
end type
type pb_52 from picturebutton within tabpage_1
end type
type pb_51 from picturebutton within tabpage_1
end type
type pb_50 from picturebutton within tabpage_1
end type
type pb_49 from picturebutton within tabpage_1
end type
type pb_48 from picturebutton within tabpage_1
end type
```

```
type pb_47 from picturebutton within tabpage_1
end type
type pb_46 from picturebutton within tabpage_1
end type
type pb_45 from picturebutton within tabpage_1
end type
type pb_44 from picturebutton within tabpage_1
end type
type pb_43 from picturebutton within tabpage_1
end type
type pb_42 from picturebutton within tabpage_1
end type
type pb_41 from picturebutton within tabpage_1
end type
type pb_35 from picturebutton within tabpage_1
end type
type pb_33 from picturebutton within tabpage_1
end type
type pb_32 from picturebutton within tabpage_1
end type
type pb_31 from picturebutton within tabpage_1
end type
type pb_30 from picturebutton within tabpage_1
end type
type pb_29 from picturebutton within tabpage_1
end type
type pb_27 from picturebutton within tabpage_1
end type
type pb_26 from picturebutton within tabpage_1
end type
type pb_25 from picturebutton within tabpage_1
end type
type pb_24 from picturebutton within tabpage_1
end type
type pb_23 from picturebutton within tabpage_1
end type
type pb_22 from picturebutton within tabpage_1
```

```
end type
type pb_21 from picturebutton within tabpage_1
end type
type pb_20 from picturebutton within tabpage_1
end type
type pb_19 from picturebutton within tabpage_1
end type
type pb_18 from picturebutton within tabpage_1
end type
type pb_13 from picturebutton within tabpage_1
end type
type pb_12 from picturebutton within tabpage_1
end type
type pb_11 from picturebutton within tabpage_1
end type
type pb_10 from picturebutton within tabpage_1
end type
type pb_9 from picturebutton within tabpage_1
end type
type pb_8 from picturebutton within tabpage_1
end type
type pb_7 from picturebutton within tabpage_1
end type
type pb_2 from picturebutton within tabpage_1
end type
type gb_2 from groupbox within tabpage_1
end type
type gb_5 from groupbox within tabpage_1
end type
type pb_28 from picturebutton within tabpage_1
end type
type gb_3 from groupbox within tabpage_1
end type
type gb_4 from groupbox within tabpage_1
end type
type tabpage_1 from userobject within tab_1
pb_69 pb_69
```

pb_63 pb_63
pb_75 pb_75
pb_74 pb_74
pb_71 pb_71
pb_68 pb_68
pb_67 pb_67
pb_66 pb_66
pb_65 pb_65
pb_64 pb_64
pb_62 pb_62
pb_61 pb_61
pb_60 pb_60
pb_57 pb_57
pb_56 pb_56
pb_55 pb_55
pb_54 pb_54
pb_53 pb_53
pb_52 pb_52
pb_51 pb_51
pb_50 pb_50
pb_49 pb_49
pb_48 pb_48
pb_47 pb_47
pb_46 pb_46
pb_45 pb_45
pb_44 pb_44
pb_43 pb_43
pb_42 pb_42
pb_41 pb_41
pb_35 pb_35
pb_33 pb_33
pb_32 pb_32
pb_31 pb_31
pb_30 pb_30
pb_29 pb_29
pb_27 pb_27
pb_26 pb_26

```
pb_25 pb_25
pb_24 pb_24
pb_23 pb_23
pb_22 pb_22
pb_21 pb_21
pb_20 pb_20
pb_19 pb_19
pb_18 pb_18
pb_13 pb_13
pb_12 pb_12
pb_11 pb_11
pb_10 pb_10
pb_9 pb_9
pb_8 pb_8
pb_7 pb_7
pb_2 pb_2
gb_2 gb_2
gb_5 gb_5
pb_28 pb_28
gb_3 gb_3
gb_4 gb_4
end type
type tabpage_5 from userobject within tab_1
end type
type pb_59 from picturebutton within tabpage_5
end type
type pb_58 from picturebutton within tabpage_5
end type
type pb_14 from picturebutton within tabpage_5
end type
type pb_6 from picturebutton within tabpage_5
end type
type pb_17 from picturebutton within tabpage_5
end type
type pb_5 from picturebutton within tabpage_5
end type
type pb_16 from picturebutton within tabpage_5
```

```
end type
type pb_4 from picturebutton within tabpage_5
end type
type pb_15 from picturebutton within tabpage_5
end type
type pb_3 from picturebutton within tabpage_5
end type
type pb_40 from picturebutton within tabpage_5
end type
type pb_39 from picturebutton within tabpage_5
end type
type pb_38 from picturebutton within tabpage_5
end type
type pb_37 from picturebutton within tabpage_5
end type
type pb_36 from picturebutton within tabpage_5
end type
type pb_34 from picturebutton within tabpage_5
end type
type pb_130 from picturebutton within tabpage_5
end type
type pb_813 from picturebutton within tabpage_5
end type
type pb_80 from picturebutton within tabpage_5
end type
type pb_79 from picturebutton within tabpage_5
end type
type pb_78 from picturebutton within tabpage_5
end type
type pb_76 from picturebutton within tabpage_5
end type
type pb_73 from picturebutton within tabpage_5
end type
type pb_72 from picturebutton within tabpage_5
end type
type pb_70 from picturebutton within tabpage_5
end type
```

```
type gb_1 from groupbox within tabpage_5
end type
type tabpage_5 from userobject within tab_1
pb_59 pb_59
pb_58 pb_58
pb_14 pb_14
pb_6 pb_6
pb_17 pb_17
pb_5 pb_5
pb_16 pb_16
pb_4 pb_4
pb_15 pb_15
pb_3 pb_3
pb_40 pb_40
pb_39 pb_39
pb_38 pb_38
pb_37 pb_37
pb_36 pb_36
pb_34 pb_34
pb_130 pb_130
pb_813 pb_813
pb_80 pb_80
pb_79 pb_79
pb_78 pb_78
pb_76 pb_76
pb_73 pb_73
pb_72 pb_72
pb_70 pb_70
gb_1 gb_1
end type
type tab_1 from tab within w_mastermenu
tabpage_1 tabpage_1
tabpage_5 tabpage_5
end type
type sle_1 from picturebutton within w_mastermenu
end type
type st_time from statictext within w_mastermenu
```

```
end type
type sle_2 from picturebutton within w_mastermenu
end type
type pb_1 from picturebutton within w_mastermenu
end type
type dw_2 from datawindow within w_mastermenu
end type
end forward
global type w_mastermenu from window
integer width = 3657
integer height = 2312
boolean titlebar = true
string title = "Good Health Plan"
string menuname = "m_menu"
boolean controlmenu = true
boolean minbox = true
long backcolor = 12639424
string icon = "Ghpllco.ico"
boolean toolbarvisible = false
dw_3 dw_3
dw_1 dw_1
tab_1 tab_1
sle_1 sle_1
st_time st_time
sle_2 sle_2
pb_1 pb_1
dw_2 dw_2
end type
global w_mastermenu w_mastermenu
type variables
end variables
on w_mastermenu.create
if this.MenuName = "m_menu" then
this.MenuID = create m_menu
this.dw_3=create dw_3
```

```
this.dw_1=create dw_1
this.tab_1=create tab_1
this.sle_1=create sle_1
this.st_time=create st_time
this.sle_2=create sle_2
this.pb_1=create pb_1
this.dw_2=create dw_2
this.Control[]={this.dw_3,&
this.dw_1,&
this.tab_1,&
this.sle_1,&
this.st_time,&
this.sle_2,&
this.pb_1,&
this.dw_2}
end on
on w_mastermenu.destroy
if IsValid(MenuID) then destroy(MenuID)
destroy(this.dw_3)
destroy(this.dw_1)
destroy(this.tab_1)
destroy(this.sle_1)
destroy(this.st_time)
destroy(this.sle_2)
destroy(this.pb_1)
destroy(this.dw_2)
end on
event open;if isvalid(w_about) then close(w_about)
st_time.Text = String(Now(), "hh:mm:ss")
Timer(1)
sle_2.text=pname
this.x=0
this.y=0
tab_1.x=0
tab_1.y=0
```

```
//close(w_login)
title=BRANCH +' - '+coname//+'-Fianancial Year '+
fayear+'('+string(finyear)+')'
module='fin'
if isvalid(w_about) then close(w_about)
if mod(day(today()),2)=0  then
sle_1.disabledname="ghplLongAni.gif"
sle_1.disabledname="DevRkAni.gif"
st_time.TEXTcolor=rgb(255,0,rand(255))
st_time.TEXTcolor=rgb(rand(255),0,255)
st_time.TEXTcolor=rgb(rand(255),255,0)
sle_1.disabledname="ghplLongAni.gif"
sle_1.disabledname="ghplLongAni.gif"
sle_1.disabledname="ghplLongAni.gif"
sle_1.disabledname="DevRkAni.gif"
case 1
case 2
case 3
case 4
case 5
case 6
module='pay'
end choose
end event
event getfocus;sle_1.enabled=false
end event
type tabpage_1 from userobject within tab_1
integer x = 18
integer y = 136
integer width = 3602
integer height = 1844
long backcolor = 134217747
string pointer = "H_NODROP.CUR"
string text = "Health Insurance"
long tabtextcolor = 33554432
```

long tabbackcolor = 12639424
long picturemaskcolor = 536870912
pb_69 pb_69
pb_63 pb_63
pb_75 pb_75
pb_74 pb_74
pb_71 pb_71
pb_68 pb_68
pb_67 pb_67
pb_66 pb_66
pb_65 pb_65
pb_64 pb_64
pb_62 pb_62
pb_61 pb_61
pb_60 pb_60
pb_57 pb_57
pb_56 pb_56
pb_55 pb_55
pb_54 pb_54
pb_53 pb_53
pb_52 pb_52
pb_51 pb_51
pb_50 pb_50
pb_49 pb_49
pb_48 pb_48
pb_47 pb_47
pb_46 pb_46
pb_45 pb_45
pb_44 pb_44
pb_43 pb_43
pb_42 pb_42
pb_41 pb_41
pb_35 pb_35
pb_33 pb_33
pb_32 pb_32

```
pb_31 pb_31
pb_30 pb_30
pb_29 pb_29
pb_27 pb_27
pb_26 pb_26
pb_25 pb_25
pb_24 pb_24
pb_23 pb_23
pb_22 pb_22
pb_21 pb_21
pb_20 pb_20
pb_19 pb_19
pb_18 pb_18
pb_13 pb_13
pb_12 pb_12
pb_11 pb_11
pb_10 pb_10
pb_9 pb_9
pb_8 pb_8
pb_7 pb_7
pb_2 pb_2
gb_2 gb_2
gb_5 gb_5
pb_28 pb_28
gb_3 gb_3
gb_4 gb_4
end type
on tabpage_1.create
this.pb_69=create pb_69
this.pb_63=create pb_63
this.pb_75=create pb_75
this.pb_74=create pb_74
this.pb_71=create pb_71
this.pb_68=create pb_68
this.pb_67=create pb_67
```

```
this.pb_66=create pb_66
this.pb_65=create pb_65
this.pb_64=create pb_64
this.pb_62=create pb_62
this.pb_61=create pb_61
this.pb_60=create pb_60
this.pb_57=create pb_57
this.pb_56=create pb_56
this.pb_55=create pb_55
this.pb_54=create pb_54
this.pb_53=create pb_53
this.pb_52=create pb_52
this.pb_51=create pb_51
this.pb_50=create pb_50
this.pb_49=create pb_49
this.pb_48=create pb_48
this.pb_47=create pb_47
this.pb_46=create pb_46
this.pb_45=create pb_45
this.pb_44=create pb_44
this.pb_43=create pb_43
this.pb_42=create pb_42
this.pb_41=create pb_41
this.pb_35=create pb_35
this.pb_33=create pb_33
this.pb_32=create pb_32
this.pb_31=create pb_31
this.pb_30=create pb_30
this.pb_29=create pb_29
this.pb_27=create pb_27
this.pb_26=create pb_26
this.pb_25=create pb_25
this.pb_24=create pb_24
this.pb_23=create pb_23
this.pb_22=create pb_22
```

```
this.pb_21=create pb_21
this.pb_20=create pb_20
this.pb_19=create pb_19
this.pb_18=create pb_18
this.pb_13=create pb_13
this.pb_12=create pb_12
this.pb_11=create pb_11
this.pb_10=create pb_10
this.pb_9=create pb_9
this.pb_8=create pb_8
this.pb_7=create pb_7
this.pb_2=create pb_2
this.gb_2=create gb_2
this.gb_5=create gb_5
this.pb_28=create pb_28
this.gb_3=create gb_3
this.gb_4=create gb_4
this.Control[]={this.pb_69,&
this.pb_63,&
this.pb_75,&
this.pb_74,&
this.pb_71,&
this.pb_68,&
this.pb_67,&
this.pb_66,&
this.pb_65,&
this.pb_64,&
this.pb_62,&
this.pb_61,&
this.pb_60,&
this.pb_57,&
this.pb_56,&
this.pb_55,&
this.pb_54,&
this.pb_53,&
```

```
this.pb_52,&
this.pb_51,&
this.pb_50,&
this.pb_49,&
this.pb_48,&
this.pb_47,&
this.pb_46,&
this.pb_45,&
this.pb_44,&
this.pb_43,&
this.pb_42,&
this.pb_41,&
this.pb_35,&
this.pb_33,&
this.pb_32,&
this.pb_31,&
this.pb_30,&
this.pb_29,&
this.pb_27,&
this.pb_26,&
this.pb_25,&
this.pb_24,&
this.pb_23,&
this.pb_22,&
this.pb_21,&
this.pb_20,&
this.pb_19,&
this.pb_18,&
this.pb_13,&
this.pb_12,&
this.pb_11,&
this.pb_10,&
this.pb_9,&
this.pb_8,&
this.pb_7,&
```

```
this.pb_2,&
this.gb_2,&
this.gb_5,&
this.pb_28,&
this.gb_3,&
this.gb_4}
end on
on tabpage_1.destroy
destroy(this.pb_69)
destroy(this.pb_63)
destroy(this.pb_75)
destroy(this.pb_74)
destroy(this.pb_71)
destroy(this.pb_68)
destroy(this.pb_67)
destroy(this.pb_66)
destroy(this.pb_65)
destroy(this.pb_64)
destroy(this.pb_62)
destroy(this.pb_61)
destroy(this.pb_60)
destroy(this.pb_57)
destroy(this.pb_56)
destroy(this.pb_55)
destroy(this.pb_54)
destroy(this.pb_53)
destroy(this.pb_52)
destroy(this.pb_51)
destroy(this.pb_50)
destroy(this.pb_49)
destroy(this.pb_48)
destroy(this.pb_47)
destroy(this.pb_46)
destroy(this.pb_45)
destroy(this.pb_44)
```

```
destroy(this.pb_43)
destroy(this.pb_42)
destroy(this.pb_41)
destroy(this.pb_35)
destroy(this.pb_33)
destroy(this.pb_32)
destroy(this.pb_31)
destroy(this.pb_30)
destroy(this.pb_29)
destroy(this.pb_27)
destroy(this.pb_26)
destroy(this.pb_25)
destroy(this.pb_24)
destroy(this.pb_23)
destroy(this.pb_22)
destroy(this.pb_21)
destroy(this.pb_20)
destroy(this.pb_19)
destroy(this.pb_18)
destroy(this.pb_13)
destroy(this.pb_12)
destroy(this.pb_11)
destroy(this.pb_10)
destroy(this.pb_9)
destroy(this.pb_8)
destroy(this.pb_7)
destroy(this.pb_2)
destroy(this.gb_2)
destroy(this.gb_5)
destroy(this.pb_28)
destroy(this.gb_3)
destroy(this.gb_4)
end on
type pb_69 from picturebutton within tabpage_1
integer x = 128
```

```
integer y = 1080
integer width = 649
integer height = 132
integer taborder = 90
integer textsize = -9
integer weight = 700
fontcharset fontcharset = ansi!
fontpitch fontpitch = variable!
fontfamily fontfamily = swiss!
string facename = "Tahoma"
string pointer = "HARROW.CUR"
string text = "AB Branch Address"
string picturename = "YelloBGround.jpg"
string disabledname = "PinkBG.jpg"
vtextalign vtextalign = vcenter!
end type
event clicked;open(w_add_ab_branch)
end event
type pb_63 from picturebutton within tabpage_1
integer x = 1463
integer y = 60
integer width = 649
integer height = 132
integer taborder = 80
integer textsize = -9
integer weight = 700
fontcharset fontcharset = ansi!
fontpitch fontpitch = variable!
fontfamily fontfamily = swiss!
string facename = "Tahoma"
string pointer = "HARROW.CUR"
string text = "Ind.Policy(United)"
string picturename = "VioletBG.jpg"
string disabledname = "PinkBG.jpg"
vtextalign vtextalign = vcenter!
```

```
end type
event clicked;if left(g_login,2)='00' or
left(g_login,2)='TI' or  left(g_login,2)='RU' then
open(w_policy_ren_uic)
end if
end event
type pb_75 from picturebutton within tabpage_1
integer x = 2130
integer y = 60
integer width = 649
integer height = 132
integer taborder = 50
integer textsize = -9
integer weight = 700
fontcharset fontcharset = ansi!
fontpitch fontpitch = variable!
fontfamily fontfamily = swiss!
string facename = "Tahoma"
string pointer = "HARROW.CUR"
string text = "Corp.Policies-ABank"
string picturename = "VioletBG.jpg"
string disabledname = "PinkBG.jpg"
vtextalign vtextalign = vcenter!
end type
event clicked;open(w_policy_corp_ab)
end event
type pb_74 from picturebutton within tabpage_1
integer x = 2130
integer y = 188
integer width = 649
integer height = 132
integer taborder = 40
integer textsize = -9
integer weight = 700
fontcharset fontcharset = ansi!
```

```
fontpitch fontpitch = variable!
fontfamily fontfamily = swiss!
string facename = "Tahoma"
string pointer = "HARROW.CUR"
string text = "Corp.Ren.Additions1"
string picturename = "VioletBG.jpg"
string disabledname = "PinkBG.jpg"
vtextalign vtextalign = vcenter!
end type
event clicked;open(w_policy_corp_ren_all_1a)
end event
type pb_71 from picturebutton within tabpage_1
integer x = 1463
integer y = 1080
integer width = 649
integer height = 132
integer taborder = 170
integer textsize = -9
integer weight = 700
fontcharset fontcharset = ansi!
fontpitch fontpitch = variable!
fontfamily fontfamily = swiss!
string facename = "Tahoma"
string pointer = "HARROW.CUR"
string text = "Arogyadhan ID Cards"
string picturename = "YelloBGround.jpg"
string disabledname = "PinkBG.jpg"
vtextalign vtextalign = vcenter!
end type
event clicked;open(w_ghpl_ids_corp_ad)
end event
type pb_68 from picturebutton within tabpage_1
integer x = 795
integer y = 1080
integer width = 649
```

```
integer height = 132
integer taborder = 160
integer textsize = -9
integer weight = 700
fontcharset fontcharset = ansi!
fontpitch fontpitch = variable!
fontfamily fontfamily = swiss!
string facename = "Tahoma"
string pointer = "HARROW.CUR"
string text = "Add-Covering Letter"
string picturename = "YelloBGround.jpg"
string disabledname = "PinkBG.jpg"
vtextalign vtextalign = vcenter!
end type
event clicked;open(w_ghpl_add_det)
end event
type pb_67 from picturebutton within tabpage_1
integer x = 2130
integer y = 444
integer width = 649
integer height = 132
integer taborder = 80
integer textsize = -9
integer weight = 700
fontcharset fontcharset = ansi!
fontpitch fontpitch = variable!
fontfamily fontfamily = swiss!
string facename = "Tahoma"
string pointer = "HARROW.CUR"
string text = "Corp.Ren.Additions3"
string picturename = "VioletBG.jpg"
string disabledname = "PinkBG.jpg"
vtextalign vtextalign = vcenter!
end type
event clicked;open(w_policy_corp_ren_all_1B)
```

```
end event
type pb_66 from picturebutton within tabpage_1
integer x = 1463
integer y = 444
integer width = 649
integer height = 132
integer taborder = 70
integer textsize = -8
integer weight = 700
fontcharset fontcharset = ansi!
fontpitch fontpitch = variable!
fontfamily fontfamily = swiss!
string facename = "Tahoma"
string pointer = "HARROW.CUR"
string text = "Corp.Pol.Renew-All-3rd"
string picturename = "VioletBG.jpg"
string disabledname = "PinkBG.jpg"
vtextalign vtextalign = vcenter!
end type
event clicked;open(w_policy_corp_ren_all_3)
end event
type pb_65 from picturebutton within tabpage_1
integer x = 795
integer y = 444
integer width = 649
integer height = 132
integer taborder = 70
integer textsize = -8
integer weight = 700
fontcharset fontcharset = ansi!
fontpitch fontpitch = variable!
fontfamily fontfamily = swiss!
string facename = "Tahoma"
string pointer = "HARROW.CUR"
string text = "Corp.Policy Renew-3rd"
```

```
string picturename = "VioletBG.jpg"
string disabledname = "PinkBG.jpg"
vtextalign vtextalign = vcenter!
end type
event clicked;open(w_policy_corp_ren_3)
end event
type pb_64 from picturebutton within tabpage_1
integer x = 128
integer y = 444
integer width = 649
integer height = 132
integer taborder = 80
integer textsize = -8
integer weight = 700
fontcharset fontcharset = ansi!
fontpitch fontpitch = variable!
fontfamily fontfamily = swiss!
string facename = "Tahoma"
string pointer = "HARROW.CUR"
string text = "Ind.Policy Renew-3rd"
string picturename = "VioletBG.jpg"
string disabledname = "PinkBG.jpg"
vtextalign vtextalign = vcenter!
end type
event clicked;open(w_policy_ren_3)
end event
type pb_62 from picturebutton within tabpage_1
integer x = 2130
integer y = 316
integer width = 649
integer height = 132
integer taborder = 70
integer textsize = -9
integer weight = 700
fontcharset fontcharset = ansi!
```

```
fontpitch fontpitch = variable!
fontfamily fontfamily = swiss!
string facename = "Tahoma"
string pointer = "HARROW.CUR"
string text = "Corp.Ren.Additions2"
string picturename = "VioletBG.jpg"
string disabledname = "PinkBG.jpg"
vtextalign vtextalign = vcenter!
end type
event clicked;open(w_policy_corp_ren_all_1)
end event
type pb_61 from picturebutton within tabpage_1
integer x = 128
integer y = 316
integer width = 649
integer height = 132
integer taborder = 70
integer textsize = -8
integer weight = 700
fontcharset fontcharset = ansi!
fontpitch fontpitch = variable!
fontfamily fontfamily = swiss!
string facename = "Tahoma"
string pointer = "HARROW.CUR"
string text = "Ind.Policy Renew-2nd"
string picturename = "VioletBG.jpg"
string disabledname = "PinkBG.jpg"
vtextalign vtextalign = vcenter!
end type
event clicked;open(w_policy_ren_2)
end event
type pb_60 from picturebutton within tabpage_1
integer x = 2130
integer y = 1080
integer width = 649
```

```
integer height = 132
integer taborder = 200
integer textsize = -8
integer weight = 700
fontcharset fontcharset = ansi!
fontpitch fontpitch = variable!
fontfamily fontfamily = swiss!
string facename = "Tahoma"
string pointer = "HARROW.CUR"
string text = " Andhra Bank Covers Ren"
string picturename = "YelloBGround.jpg"
string disabledname = "PinkBG.jpg"
vtextalign vtextalign = vcenter!
end type
event clicked;open(w_ghpl_add_corp_abg_ren)
end event
type pb_57 from picturebutton within tabpage_1
integer x = 795
integer y = 316
integer width = 649
integer height = 132
integer taborder = 60
integer textsize = -8
integer weight = 700
fontcharset fontcharset = ansi!
fontpitch fontpitch = variable!
fontfamily fontfamily = swiss!
string facename = "Tahoma"
string pointer = "HARROW.CUR"
string text = "Corp.Policy Renew-2nd"
string picturename = "VioletBG.jpg"
string disabledname = "PinkBG.jpg"
vtextalign vtextalign = vcenter!
end type
event clicked;open(w_policy_corp_ren_2)
```

```
end event
type pb_56 from picturebutton within tabpage_1
integer x = 1463
integer y = 316
integer width = 649
integer height = 132
integer taborder = 60
integer textsize = -8
integer weight = 700
fontcharset fontcharset = ansi!
fontpitch fontpitch = variable!
fontfamily fontfamily = swiss!
string facename = "Tahoma"
string pointer = "HARROW.CUR"
string text = "Corp.Pol.Renew-All-2nd"
string picturename = "VioletBG.jpg"
string disabledname = "PinkBG.jpg"
vtextalign vtextalign = vcenter!
end type
event clicked;open(w_policy_corp_ren_all_2)
end event
type pb_55 from picturebutton within tabpage_1
integer x = 128
integer y = 1680
integer width = 649
integer height = 132
integer taborder = 210
integer textsize = -9
integer weight = 700
fontcharset fontcharset = ansi!
fontpitch fontpitch = variable!
fontfamily fontfamily = swiss!
string facename = "Tahoma"
string pointer = "HARROW.CUR"
string text = "PA Request"
```

```
string picturename = "YelloBGround.jpg"
string disabledname = "PinkBG.jpg"
vtextalign vtextalign = vcenter!
end type
event clicked;open(w_ref_rep)
end event
type pb_54 from picturebutton within tabpage_1
integer x = 795
integer y = 1680
integer width = 649
integer height = 132
integer taborder = 210
integer textsize = -9
integer weight = 700
fontcharset fontcharset = ansi!
fontpitch fontpitch = variable!
fontfamily fontfamily = swiss!
string facename = "Tahoma"
string pointer = "HARROW.CUR"
string text = "Missing Pol.Nos"
string picturename = "YelloBGround.jpg"
string disabledname = "PinkBG.jpg"
vtextalign vtextalign = vcenter!
end type
event clicked;open(wr_miss)
end event
type pb_53 from picturebutton within tabpage_1
integer x = 2798
integer y = 940
integer width = 649
integer height = 132
integer taborder = 220
integer textsize = -9
integer weight = 700
fontcharset fontcharset = ansi!
```

```
fontpitch fontpitch = variable!
fontfamily fontfamily = swiss!
string facename = "Tahoma"
string pointer = "HARROW.CUR"
string text = "Corp.IDC Emp(Ren)"
string picturename = "YelloBGround.jpg"
string disabledname = "PinkBG.jpg"
vtextalign vtextalign = vcenter!
end type
event clicked;open(w_ghpl_ids_corp_empno_ren)
end event
type pb_52 from picturebutton within tabpage_1
integer x = 2130
integer y = 800
integer width = 649
integer height = 132
integer taborder = 210
integer textsize = -9
integer weight = 700
fontcharset fontcharset = ansi!
fontpitch fontpitch = variable!
fontfamily fontfamily = swiss!
string facename = "Tahoma"
string pointer = "HARROW.CUR"
string text = "Corp.IDC Indv(Ren)"
string picturename = "YelloBGround.jpg"
string disabledname = "PinkBG.jpg"
vtextalign vtextalign = vcenter!
end type
event clicked;open(w_ghpl_ids_corp_i_ren)
end event
type pb_51 from picturebutton within tabpage_1
integer x = 1463
integer y = 800
integer width = 649
```

```
integer height = 132
integer taborder = 200
integer textsize = -9
integer weight = 700
fontcharset fontcharset = ansi!
fontpitch fontpitch = variable!
fontfamily fontfamily = swiss!
string facename = "Tahoma"
string pointer = "HARROW.CUR"
string text = "Corp.ID Cards(Ren)"
string picturename = "YelloBGround.jpg"
string disabledname = "PinkBG.jpg"
vtextalign vtextalign = vcenter!
end type
event clicked;open(w_ghpl_ids_corp_ren)
end event
type pb_50 from picturebutton within tabpage_1
integer x = 2130
integer y = 940
integer width = 649
integer height = 132
integer taborder = 190
integer textsize = -9
integer weight = 700
fontcharset fontcharset = ansi!
fontpitch fontpitch = variable!
fontfamily fontfamily = swiss!
string facename = "Tahoma"
string pointer = "HARROW.CUR"
string text = "Corp.Covers(Ren)"
string picturename = "YelloBGround.jpg"
string disabledname = "PinkBG.jpg"
vtextalign vtextalign = vcenter!
end type
event clicked;open(w_ghpl_add_corp_ren)
```

```
end event
type pb_49 from picturebutton within tabpage_1
integer x = 795
integer y = 940
integer width = 649
integer height = 132
integer taborder = 270
integer textsize = -9
integer weight = 700
fontcharset fontcharset = ansi!
fontpitch fontpitch = variable!
fontfamily fontfamily = swiss!
string facename = "Tahoma"
string pointer = "HARROW.CUR"
string text = "Address Print(Ren)"
string picturename = "YelloBGround.jpg"
string disabledname = "PinkBG.jpg"
vtextalign vtextalign = vcenter!
end type
event clicked;open(w_ghpl_add_ren)
end event
type pb_48 from picturebutton within tabpage_1
integer x = 795
integer y = 800
integer width = 649
integer height = 132
integer taborder = 190
integer textsize = -9
integer weight = 700
fontcharset fontcharset = ansi!
fontpitch fontpitch = variable!
fontfamily fontfamily = swiss!
string facename = "Tahoma"
string pointer = "HARROW.CUR"
string text = "ID Cards lvnd.(Ren)"
```

```
string picturename = "YelloBGround.jpg"
string disabledname = "PinkBG.jpg"
vtextalign vtextalign = vcenter!
end type
event clicked;open(w_ghpl_ids_ind_ren)
end event
type pb_47 from picturebutton within tabpage_1
integer x = 128
integer y = 800
integer width = 649
integer height = 132
integer taborder = 200
integer textsize = -9
integer weight = 700
fontcharset fontcharset = ansi!
fontpitch fontpitch = variable!
fontfamily fontfamily = swiss!
string facename = "Tahoma"
string pointer = "HARROW.CUR"
string text = "ID Cards(Ren)"
string picturename = "YelloBGround.jpg"
string disabledname = "PinkBG.jpg"
vtextalign vtextalign = vcenter!
end type
event clicked;open(w_ghpl_ids_ren)
end event
type pb_46 from picturebutton within tabpage_1
integer x = 1463
integer y = 188
integer width = 649
integer height = 132
integer taborder = 120
integer textsize = -8
integer weight = 700
fontcharset fontcharset = ansi!
```

```
fontpitch fontpitch = variable!
fontfamily fontfamily = swiss!
string facename = "Tahoma"
string pointer = "HARROW.CUR"
string text = "Corp.Pol. Renew-All-1"
string picturename = "VioletBG.jpg"
string disabledname = "PinkBG.jpg"
vtextalign vtextalign = vcenter!
end type
event clicked;open(w_policy_corp_ren_all)
end event
type pb_45 from picturebutton within tabpage_1
integer x = 795
integer y = 188
integer width = 649
integer height = 132
integer taborder = 120
integer textsize = -9
integer weight = 700
fontcharset fontcharset = ansi!
fontpitch fontpitch = variable!
fontfamily fontfamily = swiss!
string facename = "Tahoma"
string pointer = "HARROW.CUR"
string text = "Corp.Policy Renew-1"
string picturename = "VioletBG.jpg"
string disabledname = "PinkBG.jpg"
vtextalign vtextalign = vcenter!
end type
event clicked;open(w_policy_corp_ren)
end event
type pb_44 from picturebutton within tabpage_1
integer x = 2130
integer y = 1684
integer width = 649
```

```
integer height = 132
integer taborder = 260
integer textsize = -9
integer weight = 700
fontcharset fontcharset = ansi!
fontpitch fontpitch = variable!
fontfamily fontfamily = swiss!
string facename = "Tahoma"
string pointer = "HARROW.CUR"
string text = "Claim Reports(To.Dt)"
string picturename = "YelloBGround.jpg"
string disabledname = "PinkBG.jpg"
vtextalign vtextalign = vcenter!
end type
event clicked;open(wr_claim_settled_new)
end event
type pb_43 from picturebutton within tabpage_1
integer x = 1463
integer y = 1676
integer width = 649
integer height = 132
integer taborder = 200
integer textsize = -9
integer weight = 700
fontcharset fontcharset = ansi!
fontpitch fontpitch = variable!
fontfamily fontfamily = swiss!
string facename = "Tahoma"
string pointer = "HARROW.CUR"
string text = "Claims Status"
string picturename = "YelloBGround.jpg"
string disabledname = "PinkBG.jpg"
vtextalign vtextalign = vcenter!
end type
event clicked;open(w_listaccodes_new)
```

end event

type pb_42 from picturebutton within tabpage_1

integer x = 795

integer y = 660

integer width = 649

integer height = 132

integer taborder = 190

integer textsize = -9

integer weight = 700

fontcharset fontcharset = ansi!

fontpitch fontpitch = variable!

fontfamily fontfamily = swiss!

string facename = "Tahoma"

string pointer = "HARROW.CUR"

string text = "ID Cards lvnd."

string picturename = "YelloBGround.jpg"

string disabledname = "PinkBG.jpg"

vtextalign vtextalign = vcenter!

end type

event clicked;open(w_ghpl_ids_ind)

end event

type pb_41 from picturebutton within tabpage_1

integer x = 2798

integer y = 1304

integer width = 649

integer height = 132

integer taborder = 190

integer textsize = -9

integer weight = 700

fontcharset fontcharset = ansi!

fontpitch fontpitch = variable!

fontfamily fontfamily = swiss!

string facename = "Tahoma"

string pointer = "HARROW.CUR"

string text = "Settlement Letters"

```
string picturename = "YelloBGround.jpg"
string disabledname = "PinkBG.jpg"
vtextalign vtextalign = vcenter!
end type
event clicked;open(wr_settlements)
end event
type pb_35 from picturebutton within tabpage_1
integer x = 2798
integer y = 1532
integer width = 649
integer height = 132
integer taborder = 180
integer textsize = -9
integer weight = 700
fontcharset fontcharset = ansi!
fontpitch fontpitch = variable!
fontfamily fontfamily = swiss!
string facename = "Tahoma"
string pointer = "HARROW.CUR"
string text = "Float Fund Stmt."
string picturename = "YelloBGround.jpg"
string disabledname = "PinkBG.jpg"
vtextalign vtextalign = vcenter!
end type
event clicked;open(wr_fund_repl_stmt)
end event
type pb_33 from picturebutton within tabpage_1
integer x = 2798
integer y = 1684
integer width = 649
integer height = 132
integer taborder = 250
integer textsize = -9
integer weight = 700
fontcharset fontcharset = ansi!
```

```
fontpitch fontpitch = variable!
fontfamily fontfamily = swiss!
string facename = "Tahoma"
string pointer = "HARROW.CUR"
string text = "Claim Reports"
string picturename = "YelloBGround.jpg"
string disabledname = "PinkBG.jpg"
vtextalign vtextalign = vcenter!
end type
event clicked;open(wr_claim_settled)
end event
type pb_32 from picturebutton within tabpage_1
integer x = 2130
integer y = 1532
integer width = 649
integer height = 132
integer taborder = 240
integer textsize = -9
integer weight = 700
fontcharset fontcharset = ansi!
fontpitch fontpitch = variable!
fontfamily fontfamily = swiss!
string facename = "Tahoma"
string pointer = "HARROW.CUR"
string text = "Pre-Auth Reports"
string picturename = "YelloBGround.jpg"
string disabledname = "PinkBG.jpg"
vtextalign vtextalign = vcenter!
end type
event clicked;open(wr_pre_approval_disc)
end event
type pb_31 from picturebutton within tabpage_1
integer x = 1463
integer y = 1532
integer width = 649
```

```
integer height = 132
integer taborder = 230
integer textsize = -9
integer weight = 700
fontcharset fontcharset = ansi!
fontpitch fontpitch = variable!
fontfamily fontfamily = swiss!
string facename = "Tahoma"
string pointer = "HARROW.CUR"
string text = "Pre-Authorisations"
string picturename = "YelloBGround.jpg"
string disabledname = "PinkBG.jpg"
vtextalign vtextalign = vcenter!
end type
event clicked;open(wr_pre_approval)
end event
type pb_30 from picturebutton within tabpage_1
integer x = 795
integer y = 1532
integer width = 649
integer height = 132
integer taborder = 220
integer textsize = -9
integer weight = 700
fontcharset fontcharset = ansi!
fontpitch fontpitch = variable!
fontfamily fontfamily = swiss!
string facename = "Tahoma"
string pointer = "HARROW.CUR"
string text = "Premium Details"
string picturename = "YelloBGround.jpg"
string disabledname = "PinkBG.jpg"
vtextalign vtextalign = vcenter!
end type
event clicked;open(wr_premium_det)
```

end event
type pb_29 from picturebutton within tabpage_1
integer x = 128
integer y = 1532
integer width = 649
integer height = 132
integer taborder = 210
integer textsize = -9
integer weight = 700
fontcharset fontcharset = ansi!
fontpitch fontpitch = variable!
fontfamily fontfamily = swiss!
string facename = "Tahoma"
string pointer = "HARROW.CUR"
string text = "ID Cards Issued"
string picturename = "YelloBGround.jpg"
string disabledname = "PinkBG.jpg"
vtextalign vtextalign = vcenter!
end type
event clicked;open(w_id_card_issues)
end event
type pb_27 from picturebutton within tabpage_1
integer x = 2798
integer y = 1080
integer width = 649
integer height = 132
integer taborder = 180
integer textsize = -9
integer weight = 700
fontcharset fontcharset = ansi!
fontpitch fontpitch = variable!
fontfamily fontfamily = swiss!
string facename = "Tahoma"
string pointer = "HARROW.CUR"
string text = " Andhra Bank Covers"

```
string picturename = "YelloBGround.jpg"
string disabledname = "PinkBG.jpg"
vtextalign vtextalign = vcenter!
end type
event clicked;open(w_ghpl_add_corp_abg)
end event
type pb_26 from picturebutton within tabpage_1
integer x = 2130
integer y = 1304
integer width = 649
integer height = 132
integer taborder = 200
integer textsize = -9
integer weight = 700
fontcharset fontcharset = ansi!
fontpitch fontpitch = variable!
fontfamily fontfamily = swiss!
string facename = "Tahoma"
string pointer = "HARROW.CUR"
string text = "Disallowance Form"
string picturename = "YelloBGround.jpg"
string disabledname = "PinkBG.jpg"
vtextalign vtextalign = vcenter!
end type
event clicked;open(wr_claim_reps)
end event
type pb_25 from picturebutton within tabpage_1
integer x = 1463
integer y = 1304
integer width = 649
integer height = 132
integer taborder = 190
integer textsize = -9
integer weight = 700
fontcharset fontcharset = ansi!
```

```
fontpitch fontpitch = variable!
fontfamily fontfamily = swiss!
string facename = "Tahoma"
string pointer = "HARROW.CUR"
string text = "Claim Addl.Info"
string picturename = "YelloBGround.jpg"
string disabledname = "PinkBG.jpg"
vtextalign vtextalign = vcenter!
end type
event clicked;open(wr_claim_reps_addl)
end event
type pb_24 from picturebutton within tabpage_1
integer x = 128
integer y = 188
integer width = 649
integer height = 132
integer taborder = 150
integer textsize = -9
integer weight = 700
fontcharset fontcharset = ansi!
fontpitch fontpitch = variable!
fontfamily fontfamily = swiss!
string facename = "Tahoma"
string pointer = "HARROW.CUR"
string text = "Ind.Policy Renew-1"
string picturename = "VioletBG.jpg"
string disabledname = "PinkBG.jpg"
vtextalign vtextalign = vcenter!
end type
event clicked;open(w_policy_ren)
end event
type pb_23 from picturebutton within tabpage_1
integer x = 795
integer y = 1304
integer width = 649
```

```
integer height = 132
integer taborder = 190
integer textsize = -9
integer weight = 700
fontcharset fontcharset = ansi!
fontpitch fontpitch = variable!
fontfamily fontfamily = swiss!
string facename = "Tahoma"
string pointer = "HARROW.CUR"
string text = "Enhance.Letter"
string picturename = "YelloBGround.jpg"
string disabledname = "PinkBG.jpg"
vtextalign vtextalign = vcenter!
end type
event clicked;open(wr_pre_auth_reps_enh)
end event
type pb_22 from picturebutton within tabpage_1
integer x = 795
integer y = 60
integer width = 649
integer height = 132
integer taborder = 150
integer textsize = -9
integer weight = 700
fontcharset fontcharset = ansi!
fontpitch fontpitch = variable!
fontfamily fontfamily = swiss!
string facename = "Tahoma"
string pointer = "HARROW.CUR"
string text = "Corporate Policies"
string picturename = "VioletBG.jpg"
string disabledname = "PinkBG.jpg"
vtextalign vtextalign = vcenter!
end type
event clicked;open(w_policy_corp)
```

end event

type pb_21 from picturebutton within tabpage_1

integer x = 2798

integer y = 660

integer width = 649

integer height = 132

integer taborder = 100

integer textsize = -9

integer weight = 700

fontcharset fontcharset = ansi!

fontpitch fontpitch = variable!

fontfamily fontfamily = swiss!

string facename = "Tahoma"

string pointer = "HARROW.CUR"

string text = "Settlements"

string picturename = "VioletBG.jpg"

string disabledname = "PinkBG.jpg"

vtextalign vtextalign = vcenter!

end type

event clicked;open(w_settlements)

end event

type pb_20 from picturebutton within tabpage_1

integer x = 2798

integer y = 188

integer width = 649

integer height = 132

integer taborder = 60

integer textsize = -9

integer weight = 700

fontcharset fontcharset = ansi!

fontpitch fontpitch = variable!

fontfamily fontfamily = swiss!

string facename = "Tahoma"

string pointer = "HARROW.CUR"

string text = "Pre-Auth.Enhance"

```
string picturename = "VioletBG.jpg"
string disabledname = "PinkBG.jpg"
vtextalign vtextalign = vcenter!
end type
event clicked;open(w_pre_approval_enh)
end event
type pb_19 from picturebutton within tabpage_1
integer x = 128
integer y = 1304
integer width = 649
integer height = 132
integer taborder = 180
integer textsize = -9
integer weight = 700
fontcharset fontcharset = ansi!
fontpitch fontpitch = variable!
fontfamily fontfamily = swiss!
string facename = "Tahoma"
string pointer = "HARROW.CUR"
string text = "Pre-Auth.Letters"
string picturename = "YelloBGround.jpg"
string disabledname = "PinkBG.jpg"
vtextalign vtextalign = vcenter!
end type
event clicked;open(wr_pre_auth_reps)
end event
type pb_18 from picturebutton within tabpage_1
integer x = 2130
integer y = 660
integer width = 649
integer height = 132
integer taborder = 180
integer textsize = -9
integer weight = 700
fontcharset fontcharset = ansi!
```

```
fontpitch fontpitch = variable!
fontfamily fontfamily = swiss!
string facename = "Tahoma"
string pointer = "HARROW.CUR"
string text = "Corp.ID Cards Indv"
string picturename = "YelloBGround.jpg"
string disabledname = "PinkBG.jpg"
vtextalign vtextalign = vcenter!
end type
event clicked;open(w_ghpl_ids_corp_i)
end event
type pb_13 from picturebutton within tabpage_1
integer x = 1463
integer y = 940
integer width = 649
integer height = 132
integer taborder = 170
integer textsize = -9
integer weight = 700
fontcharset fontcharset = ansi!
fontpitch fontpitch = variable!
fontfamily fontfamily = swiss!
string facename = "Tahoma"
string pointer = "HARROW.CUR"
string text = "Corp.Covers"
string picturename = "YelloBGround.jpg"
string disabledname = "PinkBG.jpg"
vtextalign vtextalign = vcenter!
end type
event clicked;open(w_ghpl_add_corp)
end event
event getfocus;this.picturename="PinkBG.jpg"
end event
event losefocus;this.picturename="YelloBGround.jpg"
end event
```

```
type pb_12 from picturebutton within tabpage_1
integer x = 1463
integer y = 660
integer width = 649
integer height = 132
integer taborder = 160
integer textsize = -9
integer weight = 700
fontcharset fontcharset = ansi!
fontpitch fontpitch = variable!
fontfamily fontfamily = swiss!
string facename = "Tahoma"
string pointer = "HARROW.CUR"
string text = "Corp.ID Cards"
string picturename = "YelloBGround.jpg"
string disabledname = "PinkBG.jpg"
vtextalign vtextalign = vcenter!
end type
event clicked;open(w_ghpl_ids_corp)
end event
event getfocus;this.picturename="PinkBG.jpg"
end event
event losefocus;this.picturename="YelloBGround.jpg"
end event
type pb_11 from picturebutton within tabpage_1
integer x = 128
integer y = 940
integer width = 649
integer height = 132
integer taborder = 150
integer textsize = -9
integer weight = 700
fontcharset fontcharset = ansi!
fontpitch fontpitch = variable!
fontfamily fontfamily = swiss!
```

```
string facename = "Tahoma"
string pointer = "HARROW.CUR"
string text = "Address Print"
string picturename = "YelloBGround.jpg"
string disabledname = "PinkBG.jpg"
vtextalign vtextalign = vcenter!
end type
event clicked;open(w_ghpl_add)
end event
event getfocus;this.picturename="PinkBG.jpg"
end event
event losefocus;this.picturename="YelloBGround.jpg"
end event
type pb_10 from picturebutton within tabpage_1
integer x = 128
integer y = 660
integer width = 649
integer height = 132
integer taborder = 140
integer textsize = -9
integer weight = 700
fontcharset fontcharset = ansi!
fontpitch fontpitch = variable!
fontfamily fontfamily = swiss!
string facename = "Tahoma"
string pointer = "HARROW.CUR"
string text = "ID Cards"
string picturename = "YelloBGround.jpg"
string disabledname = "PinkBG.jpg"
vtextalign vtextalign = vcenter!
end type
event clicked;open(w_ghpl_ids)
end event
event getfocus;this.picturename="PinkBG.jpg"
end event
```

```
event losefocus;this.picturename="YelloBGround.jpg"
end event
type pb_9 from picturebutton within tabpage_1
integer x = 2798
integer y = 444
integer width = 649
integer height = 132
integer taborder = 50
integer textsize = -9
integer weight = 700
fontcharset fontcharset = ansi!
fontpitch fontpitch = variable!
fontfamily fontfamily = swiss!
string facename = "Tahoma"
string pointer = "HARROW.CUR"
string text = "Claim Processing"
string picturename = "VioletBG.jpg"
string disabledname = "PinkBG.jpg"
vtextalign vtextalign = vcenter!
end type
event getfocus;this.picturename="PinkBG.jpg"
end event
event losefocus;this.picturename="VioletBG.jpg"
end event
event clicked;open(w_claimprocessing)
end event
type pb_8 from picturebutton within tabpage_1
integer x = 2798
integer y = 308
integer width = 649
integer height = 132
integer taborder = 40
integer textsize = -9
integer weight = 700
fontcharset fontcharset = ansi!
```

```
fontpitch fontpitch = variable!
fontfamily fontfamily = swiss!
string facename = "Tahoma"
string pointer = "HARROW.CUR"
string text = "Claims"
string picturename = "VioletBG.jpg"
string disabledname = "PinkBG.jpg"
vtextalign vtextalign = vcenter!
end type
event clicked;open(w_claims)
end event
event getfocus;this.picturename="PinkBG.jpg"
end event
event losefocus;this.picturename="VioletBG.jpg"
end event
type pb_7 from picturebutton within tabpage_1
integer x = 128
integer y = 60
integer width = 649
integer height = 132
integer taborder = 20
integer textsize = -9
integer weight = 700
fontcharset fontcharset = ansi!
fontpitch fontpitch = variable!
fontfamily fontfamily = swiss!
string facename = "Tahoma"
string pointer = "HARROW.CUR"
string text = "Indv.Policy Entry"
string picturename = "VioletBG.jpg"
string disabledname = "PinkBG.jpg"
vtextalign vtextalign = vcenter!
end type
event clicked;open(w_policy)
end event
```

```
event getfocus;this.picturename="PinkBG.jpg"
end event
event losefocus;this.picturename="VioletBG.jpg"
end event
type pb_2 from picturebutton within tabpage_1
integer x = 2798
integer y = 60
integer width = 649
integer height = 132
integer taborder = 30
integer textsize = -9
integer weight = 700
fontcharset fontcharset = ansi!
fontpitch fontpitch = variable!
fontfamily fontfamily = swiss!
string facename = "Tahoma"
string pointer = "HARROW.CUR"
string text = "Pre-Authorization"
string picturename = "VioletBG.jpg"
string disabledname = "PinkBG.jpg"
vtextalign vtextalign = vcenter!
end type
event clicked;open(w_pre_authorise)
end event
event getfocus;this.picturename="PinkBG.jpg"
end event
event losefocus;this.picturename="VioletBG.jpg"
end event
type gb_2 from groupbox within tabpage_1
integer x = 41
integer width = 3520
integer height = 592
integer textsize = -11
integer weight = 700
fontcharset fontcharset = ansi!
```

```
fontpitch fontpitch = variable!
fontfamily fontfamily = swiss!
string facename = "Tahoma"
string pointer = "H_NODROP.CUR"
long textcolor = 16711935
long backcolor = 15780518
string text = "Activities"
end type
type gb_5 from groupbox within tabpage_1
integer x = 41
integer y = 1460
integer width = 3520
integer height = 368
integer taborder = 200
integer textsize = -11
integer weight = 700
fontcharset fontcharset = ansi!
fontpitch fontpitch = variable!
fontfamily fontfamily = swiss!
string facename = "Tahoma"
string pointer = "H_NODROP.CUR"
long textcolor = 16711680
long backcolor = 12639424
string text = "Reports"
end type
type pb_28 from picturebutton within tabpage_1
integer x = 2798
integer y = 800
integer width = 649
integer height = 132
integer taborder = 190
integer textsize = -9
integer weight = 700
fontcharset fontcharset = ansi!
fontpitch fontpitch = variable!
```

```
fontfamily fontfamily = swiss!
string facename = "Tahoma"
string pointer = "HARROW.CUR"
string text = "Corp.ID Cards Emp"
string picturename = "YelloBGround.jpg"
string disabledname = "PinkBG.jpg"
vtextalign vtextalign = vcenter!
end type
event clicked;open(w_ghpl_ids_corp_empno)
end event
type gb_3 from groupbox within tabpage_1
integer x = 41
integer y = 604
integer width = 3520
integer height = 620
integer textsize = -11
integer weight = 700
fontcharset fontcharset = ansi!
fontpitch fontpitch = variable!
fontfamily fontfamily = swiss!
string facename = "Tahoma"
string pointer = "H_NODROP.CUR"
long textcolor = 16711680
long backcolor = 12639424
string text = "ID CARDS ISSUES"
end type
type gb_4 from groupbox within tabpage_1
integer x = 46
integer y = 1236
integer width = 3520
integer height = 220
integer taborder = 200
integer textsize = -11
integer weight = 700
fontcharset fontcharset = ansi!
```

```
fontpitch fontpitch = variable!
fontfamily fontfamily = swiss!
string facename = "Tahoma"
string pointer = "H_NODROP.CUR"
long textcolor = 16711680
long backcolor = 15780518
string text = "Documents"
end type
type tabpage_5 from userobject within tab_1
integer x = 18
integer y = 136
integer width = 3602
integer height = 1844
long backcolor = 12639424
string pointer = "H_NODROP.CUR"
string text = "Masters"
long tabtextcolor = 33554432
long tabbackcolor = 12639424
long picturemaskcolor = 536870912
pb_59 pb_59
pb_58 pb_58
pb_14 pb_14
pb_6 pb_6
pb_17 pb_17
pb_5 pb_5
pb_16 pb_16
pb_4 pb_4
pb_15 pb_15
pb_3 pb_3
pb_40 pb_40
pb_39 pb_39
pb_38 pb_38
pb_37 pb_37
pb_36 pb_36
pb_34 pb_34
```

```
pb_130 pb_130
pb_813 pb_813
pb_80 pb_80
pb_79 pb_79
pb_78 pb_78
pb_76 pb_76
pb_73 pb_73
pb_72 pb_72
pb_70 pb_70
gb_1 gb_1
end type
on tabpage_5.create
this.pb_59=create pb_59
this.pb_58=create pb_58
this.pb_14=create pb_14
this.pb_6=create pb_6
this.pb_17=create pb_17
this.pb_5=create pb_5
this.pb_16=create pb_16
this.pb_4=create pb_4
this.pb_15=create pb_15
this.pb_3=create pb_3
this.pb_40=create pb_40
this.pb_39=create pb_39
this.pb_38=create pb_38
this.pb_37=create pb_37
this.pb_36=create pb_36
this.pb_34=create pb_34
this.pb_130=create pb_130
this.pb_813=create pb_813
this.pb_80=create pb_80
this.pb_79=create pb_79
this.pb_78=create pb_78
this.pb_76=create pb_76
this.pb_73=create pb_73
```

```
this.pb_72=create pb_72
this.pb_70=create pb_70
this.gb_1=create gb_1
this.Control[]={this.pb_59,&
this.pb_58,&
this.pb_14,&
this.pb_6,&
this.pb_17,&
this.pb_5,&
this.pb_16,&
this.pb_4,&
this.pb_15,&
this.pb_3,&
this.pb_40,&
this.pb_39,&
this.pb_38,&
this.pb_37,&
this.pb_36,&
this.pb_34,&
this.pb_130,&
this.pb_813,&
this.pb_80,&
this.pb_79,&
this.pb_78,&
this.pb_76,&
this.pb_73,&
this.pb_72,&
this.pb_70,&
this.gb_1}
end on
on tabpage_5.destroy
destroy(this.pb_59)
destroy(this.pb_58)
destroy(this.pb_14)
destroy(this.pb_6)
```

```
destroy(this.pb_17)
destroy(this.pb_5)
destroy(this.pb_16)
destroy(this.pb_4)
destroy(this.pb_15)
destroy(this.pb_3)
destroy(this.pb_40)
destroy(this.pb_39)
destroy(this.pb_38)
destroy(this.pb_37)
destroy(this.pb_36)
destroy(this.pb_34)
destroy(this.pb_130)
destroy(this.pb_813)
destroy(this.pb_80)
destroy(this.pb_79)
destroy(this.pb_78)
destroy(this.pb_76)
destroy(this.pb_73)
destroy(this.pb_72)
destroy(this.pb_70)
destroy(this.gb_1)
end on
type pb_59 from picturebutton within tabpage_5
integer x = 2770
integer y = 184
integer width = 649
integer height = 132
integer taborder = 60
integer textsize = -9
integer weight = 700
fontcharset fontcharset = ansi!
fontpitch fontpitch = variable!
fontfamily fontfamily = swiss!
string facename = "Tahoma"
```

```
string pointer = "HARROW.CUR"
string text = "Claim Status"
string picturename = "GreenishBG.jpg"
string disabledname = "PinkBG.jpg"
vtextalign vtextalign = vcenter!
end type
event clicked;open(w_cl_status)
end event
type pb_58 from picturebutton within tabpage_5
integer x = 2770
integer y = 340
integer width = 649
integer height = 132
integer taborder = 70
integer textsize = -9
integer weight = 700
fontcharset fontcharset = ansi!
fontpitch fontpitch = variable!
fontfamily fontfamily = swiss!
string facename = "Tahoma"
string pointer = "HARROW.CUR"
string text = "Disease Limits"
string picturename = "GreenishBG.jpg"
string disabledname = "PinkBG.jpg"
vtextalign vtextalign = vcenter!
end type
event clicked;open(w_disease_lim)
end event
type pb_14 from picturebutton within tabpage_5
integer x = 2103
integer y = 340
integer width = 649
integer height = 132
integer taborder = 60
integer textsize = -9
```

```
integer weight = 700
fontcharset fontcharset = ansi!
fontpitch fontpitch = variable!
fontfamily fontfamily = swiss!
string facename = "Tahoma"
string pointer = "HARROW.CUR"
string text = "Diseases"
string picturename = "GreenishBG.jpg"
string disabledname = "PinkBG.jpg"
vtextalign vtextalign = vcenter!
end type
event clicked;open(w_discase)
end event
type pb_6 from picturebutton within tabpage_5
integer x = 2103
integer y = 184
integer width = 649
integer height = 132
integer taborder = 50
integer textsize = -9
integer weight = 700
fontcharset fontcharset = ansi!
fontpitch fontpitch = variable!
fontfamily fontfamily = swiss!
string facename = "Tahoma"
string pointer = "HARROW.CUR"
string text = "Hospitals"
string picturename = "GreenishBG.jpg"
string disabledname = "PinkBG.jpg"
vtextalign vtextalign = vcenter!
end type
event clicked;open(w_hospitals)
end event
event getfocus;this.picturename="PinkBG.jpg"
end event
```

```
event losefocus;this.picturename="YelloBGround.jpg"
end event
type pb_17 from picturebutton within tabpage_5
integer x = 1435
integer y = 340
integer width = 649
integer height = 132
integer taborder = 50
integer textsize = -9
integer weight = 700
fontcharset fontcharset = ansi!
fontpitch fontpitch = variable!
fontfamily fontfamily = swiss!
string facename = "Tahoma"
string pointer = "HARROW.CUR"
string text = "Claim Items"
string picturename = "GreenishBG.jpg"
string disabledname = "PinkBG.jpg"
vtextalign vtextalign = vcenter!
end type
event clicked;open(w_cl_items)
end event
type pb_5 from picturebutton within tabpage_5
integer x = 1435
integer y = 184
integer width = 649
integer height = 132
integer taborder = 40
integer textsize = -9
integer weight = 700
fontcharset fontcharset = ansi!
fontpitch fontpitch = variable!
fontfamily fontfamily = swiss!
string facename = "Tahoma"
string pointer = "HARROW.CUR"
```

```
string text = "Ins.Co.Branches"
string picturename = "GreenishBG.jpg"
string disabledname = "PinkBG.jpg"
vtextalign vtextalign = vcenter!
end type
event clicked;open(w_ins_co_branch)
end event
event getfocus;this.picturename="PinkBG.jpg"
end event
event losefocus;this.picturename="GreenishBG.jpg"
end event
type pb_16 from picturebutton within tabpage_5
integer x = 768
integer y = 340
integer width = 649
integer height = 132
integer taborder = 40
integer textsize = -9
integer weight = 700
fontcharset fontcharset = ansi!
fontpitch fontpitch = variable!
fontfamily fontfamily = swiss!
string facename = "Tahoma"
string pointer = "HARROW.CUR"
string text = "Claim Check List"
string picturename = "GreenishBG.jpg"
string disabledname = "PinkBG.jpg"
vtextalign vtextalign = vcenter!
end type
event clicked;open(w_checklist)
end event
type pb_4 from picturebutton within tabpage_5
integer x = 768
integer y = 184
integer width = 649
```

```
integer height = 132
integer taborder = 30
integer textsize = -9
integer weight = 700
fontcharset fontcharset = ansi!
fontpitch fontpitch = variable!
fontfamily fontfamily = swiss!
string facename = "Tahoma"
string pointer = "HARROW.CUR"
string text = "Ins.Co.Regions"
string picturename = "GreenishBG.jpg"
string disabledname = "PinkBG.jpg"
vtextalign vtextalign = vcenter!
end type
event clicked;OPEN(w_ins_co_region)
end event
event getfocus;this.picturename="PinkBG.jpg"
end event
event losefocus;this.picturename="GreenishBG.jpg"
end event
type pb_15 from picturebutton within tabpage_5
integer x = 105
integer y = 340
integer width = 649
integer height = 132
integer taborder = 30
integer textsize = -9
integer weight = 700
fontcharset fontcharset = ansi!
fontpitch fontpitch = variable!
fontfamily fontfamily = swiss!
string facename = "Tahoma"
string pointer = "HARROW.CUR"
string text = "Corporates"
string picturename = "GreenishBG.jpg"
```

```
string disabledname = "PinkBG.jpg"
vtextalign vtextalign = vcenter!
end type
event clicked;open(w_corporates)
end event
type pb_3 from picturebutton within tabpage_5
integer x = 105
integer y = 184
integer width = 649
integer height = 132
integer taborder = 20
integer textsize = -9
integer weight = 700
fontcharset fontcharset = ansi!
fontpitch fontpitch = variable!
fontfamily fontfamily = swiss!
string facename = "Tahoma"
string pointer = "HARROW.CUR"
string text = "Corp.Premium"
string picturename = "GreenishBG.jpg"
string disabledname = "PinkBG.jpg"
vtextalign vtextalign = vcenter!
end type
event clicked;open(w_corp_premium_amt)
end event
event getfocus;this.picturename="PinkBG.jpg"
end event
event losefocus;this.picturename="GreenishBG.jpg"
end event
type pb_40 from picturebutton within tabpage_5
integer x = 2770
integer y = 876
integer width = 649
integer height = 132
integer taborder = 110
```

```
integer textsize = -9
integer weight = 700
fontcharset fontcharset = ansi!
fontpitch fontpitch = variable!
fontfamily fontfamily = swiss!
string facename = "Tahoma"
string pointer = "HARROW.CUR"
string text = "Add Photos"
string picturename = "GreenishBG.jpg"
string disabledname = "PinkBG.jpg"
vtextalign vtextalign = vcenter!
end type
event clicked;open(w_addphotos)
end event
type pb_39 from picturebutton within tabpage_5
integer x = 2103
integer y = 876
integer width = 649
integer height = 132
integer taborder = 130
integer textsize = -9
integer weight = 700
fontcharset fontcharset = ansi!
fontpitch fontpitch = variable!
fontfamily fontfamily = swiss!
string facename = "Tahoma"
string pointer = "HARROW.CUR"
string text = "Repudations"
string picturename = "GreenishBG.jpg"
string disabledname = "PinkBG.jpg"
vtextalign vtextalign = vcenter!
end type
event clicked;open(w_repudations)
end event
type pb_38 from picturebutton within tabpage_5
```

```
integer x = 1435
integer y = 876
integer width = 649
integer height = 132
integer taborder = 120
integer textsize = -9
integer weight = 700
fontcharset fontcharset = ansi!
fontpitch fontpitch = variable!
fontfamily fontfamily = swiss!
string facename = "Tahoma"
string pointer = "HARROW.CUR"
string text = "Occupations"
string picturename = "GreenishBG.jpg"
string disabledname = "PinkBG.jpg"
vtextalign vtextalign = vcenter!
end type
event clicked;open(w_occupations)
end event
type pb_37 from picturebutton within tabpage_5
integer x = 768
integer y = 876
integer width = 649
integer height = 132
integer taborder = 240
integer textsize = -9
integer weight = 700
fontcharset fontcharset = ansi!
fontpitch fontpitch = variable!
fontfamily fontfamily = swiss!
string facename = "Tahoma"
string pointer = "HARROW.CUR"
string text = "Relations"
string picturename = "GreenishBG.jpg"
string disabledname = "PinkBG.jpg"
```

```
vtextalign vtextalign = vcenter!
end type
event clicked;open(w_relations)
end event
type pb_36 from picturebutton within tabpage_5
integer x = 105
integer y = 876
integer width = 649
integer height = 132
integer taborder = 230
integer textsize = -9
integer weight = 700
fontcharset fontcharset = ansi!
fontpitch fontpitch = variable!
fontfamily fontfamily = swiss!
string facename = "Tahoma"
string pointer = "HARROW.CUR"
string text = "NOL Codes"
string picturename = "GreenishBG.jpg"
string disabledname = "PinkBG.jpg"
vtextalign vtextalign = vcenter!
end type
event clicked;open(w_nol_codes)
end event
type pb_34 from picturebutton within tabpage_5
integer x = 105
integer y = 564
integer width = 649
integer height = 132
integer taborder = 60
integer textsize = -9
integer weight = 700
fontcharset fontcharset = ansi!
fontpitch fontpitch = variable!
fontfamily fontfamily = swiss!
```

```
string facename = "Tahoma"
string pointer = "HARROW.CUR"
string text = "Users"
string picturename = "GreenishBG.jpg"
string disabledname = "PinkBG.jpg"
vtextalign vtextalign = vcenter!
end type
event clicked;//if g_login='00' then
open(w_users)
//end if
end event
event getfocus;this.picturename="PinkBG.jpg"
end event
event losefocus;this.picturename="YelloBGround.jpg"
end event
type pb_130 from picturebutton within tabpage_5
integer x = 768
integer y = 720
integer width = 649
integer height = 132
integer taborder = 230
integer textsize = -9
integer weight = 700
fontcharset fontcharset = ansi!
fontpitch fontpitch = variable!
fontfamily fontfamily = swiss!
string facename = "Tahoma"
string pointer = "HARROW.CUR"
string text = "Departments"
string picturename = "GreenishBG.jpg"
string disabledname = "PinkBG.jpg"
vtextalign vtextalign = vcenter!
end type
event clicked;open(w_departments)
end event
```

```
type pb_813 from picturebutton within tabpage_5
integer x = 105
integer y = 720
integer width = 649
integer height = 132
integer taborder = 220
integer textsize = -9
integer weight = 700
fontcharset fontcharset = ansi!
fontpitch fontpitch = variable!
fontfamily fontfamily = swiss!
string facename = "Tahoma"
string pointer = "HARROW.CUR"
string text = "District"
string picturename = "GreenishBG.jpg"
string disabledname = "PinkBG.jpg"
vtextalign vtextalign = vcenter!
end type
event clicked;open(w_dist)
end event
event getfocus;this.picturename="PinkBG.jpg"
end event
event losefocus;this.picturename="GreenishBG.jpg"
end event
type pb_80 from picturebutton within tabpage_5
integer x = 2103
integer y = 720
integer width = 649
integer height = 132
integer taborder = 120
integer textsize = -9
integer weight = 700
fontcharset fontcharset = ansi!
fontpitch fontpitch = variable!
fontfamily fontfamily = swiss!
```

```
string facename = "Tahoma"
string pointer = "HARROW.CUR"
string text = "Country"
string picturename = "GreenishBG.jpg"
string disabledname = "PinkBG.jpg"
vtextalign vtextalign = vcenter!
end type
event clicked;open(w_country)
end event
event getfocus;this.picturename="PinkBG.jpg"
end event
event losefocus;this.picturename="GreenishBG.jpg"
end event
type pb_79 from picturebutton within tabpage_5
integer x = 1435
integer y = 720
integer width = 649
integer height = 132
integer taborder = 110
integer textsize = -9
integer weight = 700
fontcharset fontcharset = ansi!
fontpitch fontpitch = variable!
fontfamily fontfamily = swiss!
string facename = "Tahoma"
string pointer = "HARROW.CUR"
string text = "State"
string picturename = "GreenishBG.jpg"
string disabledname = "PinkBG.jpg"
vtextalign vtextalign = vcenter!
end type
event clicked;open(w_state)
end event
event getfocus;this.picturename="PinkBG.jpg"
end event
```

```
event losefocus;this.picturename="GreenishBG.jpg"
end event
type pb_78 from picturebutton within tabpage_5
integer x = 2770
integer y = 720
integer width = 649
integer height = 132
integer taborder = 100
integer textsize = -9
integer weight = 700
fontcharset fontcharset = ansi!
fontpitch fontpitch = variable!
fontfamily fontfamily = swiss!
string facename = "Tahoma"
string pointer = "HARROW.CUR"
string text = "City"
string picturename = "GreenishBG.jpg"
string disabledname = "PinkBG.jpg"
vtextalign vtextalign = vcenter!
end type
event clicked;open(w_city)
end event
event getfocus;this.picturename="PinkBG.jpg"
end event
event losefocus;this.picturename="GreenishBG.jpg"
end event
type pb_76 from picturebutton within tabpage_5
integer x = 1435
integer y = 564
integer width = 649
integer height = 132
integer taborder = 80
integer textsize = -9
integer weight = 700
fontcharset fontcharset = ansi!
```

```
fontpitch fontpitch = variable!
fontfamily fontfamily = swiss!
string facename = "Tahoma"
string pointer = "HARROW.CUR"
string text = "Payment Terms"
string picturename = "GreenishBG.jpg"
string disabledname = "PinkBG.jpg"
vtextalign vtextalign = vcenter!
end type
event getfocus;this.picturename="PinkBG.jpg"
end event
event losefocus;this.picturename="GreenishBG.jpg"
end event
type pb_73 from picturebutton within tabpage_5
integer x = 2770
integer y = 564
integer width = 649
integer height = 132
integer taborder = 50
integer textsize = -9
integer weight = 700
fontcharset fontcharset = ansi!
fontpitch fontpitch = variable!
fontfamily fontfamily = swiss!
string facename = "Tahoma"
string pointer = "HARROW.CUR"
string text = "Phone Types"
string picturename = "GreenishBG.jpg"
string disabledname = "PinkBG.jpg"
vtextalign vtextalign = vcenter!
end type
event clicked;open(w_phonetype)
end event
event getfocus;this.picturename="PinkBG.jpg"
end event
```

```
event losefocus;this.picturename="GreenishBG.jpg"
end event
type pb_72 from picturebutton within tabpage_5
integer x = 768
integer y = 564
integer width = 649
integer height = 132
integer taborder = 20
integer textsize = -9
integer weight = 700
fontcharset fontcharset = ansi!
fontpitch fontpitch = variable!
fontfamily fontfamily = swiss!
string facename = "Tahoma"
string pointer = "HARROW.CUR"
string text = "Policy Types"
string picturename = "GreenishBG.jpg"
string disabledname = "PinkBG.jpg"
vtextalign vtextalign = vcenter!
end type
event clicked;open(w_pol_types)
end event
event getfocus;this.picturename="PinkBG.jpg"
end event
event losefocus;this.picturename="GreenishBG.jpg"
end event
type pb_70 from picturebutton within tabpage_5
integer x = 2103
integer y = 564
integer width = 649
integer height = 132
integer taborder = 40
integer textsize = -9
integer weight = 700
fontcharset fontcharset = ansi!
```

```
fontpitch fontpitch = variable!
fontfamily fontfamily = swiss!
string facename = "Tahoma"
string pointer = "HARROW.CUR"
string text = "Order Type"
string picturename = "GreenishBG.jpg"
string disabledname = "PinkBG.jpg"
vtextalign vtextalign = vcenter!
end type
event clicked;//open(w_ordertype)
end event
event getfocus;this.picturename="PinkBG.jpg"
end event
event losefocus;this.picturename="GreenishBG.jpg"
end event
type gb_1 from groupbox within tabpage_5
integer x = 50
integer y = 84
integer width = 3474
integer height = 944
integer textsize = -9
integer weight = 700
fontcharset fontcharset = ansi!
fontpitch fontpitch = variable!
fontfamily fontfamily = swiss!
string facename = "Tahoma"
string pointer = "H_NODROP.CUR"
long textcolor = 16711680
long backcolor = 15780518
string text = "Setup Masters"
end type
type sle_1 from picturebutton within w_mastermenu
integer y = 1980
integer width = 2171
integer height = 116
```

```
boolean bringtotop = true
integer textsize = -12
integer weight = 700
fontcharset fontcharset = ansi!
fontpitch fontpitch = variable!
fontfamily fontfamily = roman!
string facename = "Garamond"
string pointer = "HARROW.CUR"
boolean enabled = false
boolean cancel = true
boolean default = true
string picturename = "ABackground.jpg "
string disabledname = "DevRkAni.gif"
alignment htextalign = left!
vtextalign vtextalign = vcenter!
end type
event clicked;gf_messask("This Bar Shows on-Line Help",1)
end event
type st_time from statictext within w_mastermenu
integer x = 2171
integer y = 1984
integer width = 425
integer height = 112
boolean bringtotop = true
integer textsize = -16
integer weight = 700
fontcharset fontcharset = ansi!
fontpitch fontpitch = variable!
string facename = "Digiface"
string pointer = "HARROW.CUR"
long textcolor = 16711935
long backcolor = 12639424
boolean enabled = false
string text = "11:01:00"
alignment alignment = center!
```

```
boolean border = true
borderstyle borderstyle = styleraised!
boolean focusrectangle = false
end type
type sle_2 from picturebutton within w_mastermenu
integer x = 2601
integer y = 1980
integer width = 713
integer height = 124
boolean bringtotop = true
integer textsize = -12
integer weight = 700
fontcharset fontcharset = ansi!
fontpitch fontpitch = variable!
fontfamily fontfamily = roman!
string facename = "Garamond"
string pointer = "H_NODROP.CUR"
string text = "User Name"
boolean cancel = true
boolean default = true
string picturename = "ABackGround.jpg"
string disabledname = "background1.jpg"
vtextalign vtextalign = vcenter!
end type
event clicked;
//gf_messask("This Bar Shows the User Name",1)
if gf_messask("Your System will be locked",2)=1 then
w_mastermenu.enabled=false
open(w_login_cd)
w_login_cd.sle_pc.text=pname
close(parent)
MessageBox ("Cannot Connect to Database",
 sqlca.sqlerrtext)
return
pre_app_no=dw_3.getitemnumber(ctr,"pre_app_no")
```

```
  SELECT v_pre_app_enh.app_amt+
isnull( v_pre_app_enh.enh_amt ,0)
   INTO :cl_amt
   FROM v_pre_app_enh
WHERE v_pre_app_enh.pre_app_no = :pre_app_no;
dw_3.setitem(ctr,"cl_amt",cl_amt)
next
dw_3.update()
dw_3.reset()
commit;
end event
```

****

The main menu for this project

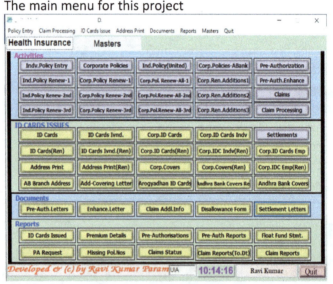

This is a small project compared to others. This application was developed using PowerBuilder 11 with sqlserver2000 on a Windows server. But maintenance was done for 10 years. As requirements and new insurance companies were added, new types of policies came, new processes were introduced by the insurance companies, and constant modifications were necessary. Either in the application or in reports.

Web Application link to download developed using visual studio 2005, combidata.bak for sqlserver 2008. These are available in the following location in zip format.

https://www.dropbox.com/s/ent1690a1kfxq1g/Web%20Application.zip?dl=0

Powerbuilder Application available at this location:

https://www.dropbox.com/s/x17g6in2bgcr987/rk_ghpl_pb11.zip?dl=0

Chapter 2

Here I will explain some of the commands that will be useful in developing software.

Datawindow commands:

Dw_1.insertrow(0) : inserts a row in datawindow dw_1

Dw_1.deletetow(rowno) marks for deletion the rowno

Dw_1.update() updates the datawindow to the table

If the status of the dw_1.getitemstatus(rowno,0,primary!) is new! the row will not be updated. If the status is NewModified the row will be inserted into the table. If the status is DataModified the row data is updated to the table. If NotModified! Nothing will happen.

Same way dw_1.setitemstatus(rowno,colno,primary!,status) can reset the status of the row or column with the status explained above.

There are many properties for datawindow which can be altered programmatically.

Dw_1.accepttext() updates the text entered in the datawindow. It will be useful when checking the data entered in the present row. Data as the entered value can be checked after passing accepttext().

Dw_1.getitem, dw_1.setitem will get the data from a column and row and set the data back to them.

Getitem has many forms based on the data type:getitemstring will retrieve a string, getitemnumber retrieves a number and getitemdate or getitemdatetime will retrieve the dates or datetime.

If you check the itemchanged event in the master windows, you will find some of the commands used there for verifying data entered.

Dw_1.getchild command is useful for manipulating the dropdowns in the datawindow and any child windows.

Dw_1.setsort("colname asc/desc") //sort is defined

Dw_1.sort() //actual sort is performed

Dw_1.setfilter("colname=value") // set to filter out data

179

Dw_1.filter() //actula filtering performed

Dw_1.getsqlselect() //sql query used in the datawindow

Dw_1.setsqlselect("sql query") // set a new sql select query

//Check datawindow control in PB help get a full list of datawindow functions.

//Same way properties can be managed by code in the runtime or program in the columns of the data window. For example, you want to manipulate the visibility of the column based on some logic. It can be coded on the datawindow itself or at the runtime in the window script.

Dw_1.describe(property list)//Use Describe to understand the structure of a DataWindow. For example, you can find out which bands the DataWindow uses and what the datatypes of the columns are. You can also use Describe to find out the current value of a property and use that value to make further modifications at runtime.

Ex: string   ls_data_type   = dw_1.Describe("salary.ColType")

It will return the column type of salary.

Datastore: Datastore is a nonvisual datawindow control. There are many uses for datastore. Holding the data in datastore can be distributed across many datawindows.

Nested objects on datawindow.

Rowscopy and rowsmove. Rows can be copied between datawindows and moved across.

****

Script for the Browse button

The script for the Browse button creates an HTML string from the data in the DataWindow by assigning the Data.HTMLTable property to a string variable. After constructing the HTML string, the script adds a header to the HTML string. Then the script saves the HTML to a file and runs the Web browser to display the output.

String ls_HTML, ls_FileName, ls_BrowserPath

```
Integer li_FileNumber, li_Bytes,
Integer li_RunResult, li_Result

// Generate the HTML from datawindow.
ls_HTML = dw_1.Object.DataWindow.Data.HTMLTable
IF IsNull(ls_HTML) Or Len(ls_HTML) <= 1 THEN
    MessageBox ("Error", "Error generating HTML!")
    Return
ELSE
    ls_HTML    ="<H1>HTML    Generated    From    a
DataWindow"&
    + "</H1><P>" + ls_HTML
END IF


//Create the file.
ls_FileName = "custlist.htm"
li_FileNumber = FileOpen(ls_FileName, StreamMode!, &
    Write!, LockReadWrite!, Replace! )

IF (li_FileNumber >= 0) THEN
    li_Bytes = FileWrite(li_FileNumber, ls_HTML)
    FileClose(li_FileNumber)
    IF li_Bytes = Len(ls_HTML) THEN
    // Run Browser with the HTML file.
    IF Not FileExists(is_Browser) THEN
        cb_selbrowser.Trigger Event Clicked()
        IF NOT FileExists(is_Browser) THEN
    MessageBox("Select Browser", "Could &
    not find the browser.")
        RETURN
        END IF
    END IF
    li_RunResult = Run(is_Browser + " file:///"+&
        ls_FileName)
    IF li_RunResult = -1 THEN
    MessageBox("Error", "Error running browser!")
        END IF
```

```
      ELSE
        MessageBox ("Write Error", &
        "File Write Unsuccessful")
      END IF
ELSE
    MessageBox ("File Error", "Could not open file")
END IF
```
****

Did you know you can run SQL commands from the windows?

You can use the paste Sql button to generate SQL commands from the tables available with the DB connection. You can even declare cursors and run them in the pb windows.

The only problem you may encounter with an MS SQL server is that you can't have two SQL commands running simultaneously. So you can use a datastore to run the second command or you can create a new transaction object and run them, which can slow the connection a little.

You can access the events and functions from the inherited master with a . notation parent.

You can even disable the parent code.

Chapter 3

PowerServer is a tool to distribute the PowerBuilder software through the internet to the users. The compiled .pbd will be stored and can be distributed to the users.

Chapter 4

.Net technology and PowerBuilder:

.Net technology was available from version 11 and it becomes more powerful day by day.

In version 11 you can convert the code to c# version and can load in an IIS server and run as a web application. There was not much control over the generated software and it was a little slow to run. But now with subsequent versions and at present version 2022Beta2, they have come up with editing the generated code for errors in the construction of the code.

It is interesting to check out this feature.

I will bring out the details of using this feature in subsequent books.

Chapter 5

Reports

There are many types of reports available with PowerBuilder.

You can prepare a report as a datawindow and put it on a window for the reports to activate and print ready.

There are many formats available for reports.

1. Composite datawindows allowed more than one datawindow to be placed on the datawindow reports.
2. the report can be retrieved with the retrieval arguments called on the main datawindow and these or any other column value can be passed on to the datawindows to retrieve the reports.
3. CrossTab Reports are useful when preparing data from multiple values. Like branches and years of data.
4. Freeform is used for the master data from a single row. This format is mainly used in data entry operations.
5. Graph is as the name suggests can prepare any type of graph from data supplied.
6. Grid is useful for letting the user have a look at the data in horizontal form and the length of the columns can be manipulated at run time. Useful for data entry or reports where data is presented in multiple rows.
7. Group reports with items grouping.
8. Label You can create Labels and print addresses and like.
9. N up The N-Up style presents two or more rows of data next to each other. It is similar to the Label style in that you can have information from several rows in the database across the page. However, the information is not meant to be printed on labels. The N-Up presentation

style is useful if you have periodic data; you can set it up so that each period repeats in a row.

10. Ole2.0 External links can be attached to the datawindows.
11. Rich text formatting can be done
12. Tabular is similar to grid, but there are no grid lines and columns can't be automatically manipulated at runtime.
13. Treeview

It is interesting to work with many formats of datawindows.

Mail Configuration in PowerBuilder:

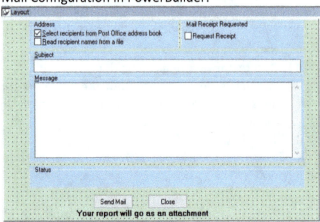

```
//open event code, so it can receive the details from the
button
dw_1 = Message.PowerObjectParm
//send mail event code
mailSession                    mSes
mailReturnCode                 mRet
mailMessage                    mMsg
mailFileDescription    mAttach
string                         ls_ret,
ls_syntax, ls_name, ls_open_pathname, ls_filename
string
        ls_attach_name='c:\DataReport.emf'
int
        li_index, li_nret, li_nrecipients, li_nfile
boolean
        lb_noerrors
```

```
If    NOT    cbx_file.checked    AND    NOT
cbx_address_live.checked Then
        MessageBox ("send Mail",    "Please    select
at least 1 address option", &

                        Exclamation!)
```

```
             wf_logoff_mail(mSes, ls_attach_name)
             return
End If

mSes = create mailSession

mRet = mSes.mailLogon ( mailNewSession! )
ls_ret = f_mail_error_to_string ( mRet, 'Logon:', FALSE )
st_status_bar.text = ' Logon: ' + ls_ret
If mRet <> mailReturnSuccess! Then
             MessageBox ("Mail Logon", 'Return Code <>
mailReturnSuccess!' )
             wf_logoff_mail(mSes, ls_attach_name)
             return
End If
SetPointer(HourGlass!)
mMsg.Subject    = mle_subject.text
If cbx_receipt_requested.checked Then
             mMsg.ReceiptRequested = true
End If
mMsg.notetext = mle_msg.text +"~n~r "
mAttach.FileType = mailAttach!
mAttach.PathName = ls_attach_name
mAttach.FileName = ls_attach_name
// Note: In MS Mail version 3.0b, Position=-1 puts
attachment at
// the beginning of the message.
// This will place the attachment at the End of the text
of the message
mAttach.Position = len(mMsg.notetext) - 1
mMsg.AttachmentFile[1] = mAttach

/**********************************************
****
If user requested "addresses-from-a-file," open that file
and
             read the address list.
```

```
************************************************
***/
If cbx_file.checked Then
        li_nret    =    GetFileOpenName    ("Address",
ls_open_pathname, &
        ls_filename,"adr", &
        "Address   Text   Files   (*.adr),*.adr,All   Files
(*.*),*.*")
        If li_nret < 1 Then return
        li_nfile = FileOpen ( ls_open_pathname )
        If li_nfile < 0 Then
        MessageBox ( "send Mail", "Unable to open file
" + ls_open_pathname, StopSign! )
wf_logoff_mail(mSes, ls_attach_name)
                return
        End If


        li_nrecipients = 0
        do while FileRead ( li_nfile, ls_name ) > 0
        li_nrecipients = li_nrecipients + 1
        mMsg.Recipient[li_nrecipients].Name            =
ls_name
        loop
        FileClose ( li_nfile )
End If

/*********************************************
****

        If user requested "address-from-Post-Office,"
call the
        mail system's Address function

************************************************
***/
If cbx_address_live.checked Then
        mRet = mSes.mailAddress ( mMsg )
```

```
        If mRet = mailReturnUserAbort! Then
            st_status_bar.text  =  "User   Canceled
send Mail"
            wf_logoff_mail(mSes, ls_attach_name)
            Return
        End If
        ls_ret = f_mail_error_to_string ( mRet, 'Address
Mail:', FALSE )
        st_status_bar.text = ' Address Mail: ' + ls_ret
End If

/********************************************
****
        Resolve recipient addresses, which may be only
partially
        supplied, to get the complete address for each
one.

        Loop in this until the names are all resovled
with no
        errors. The message will not be sent If errors
are in
        the user name.

        The user can cancel out of resolving names
which
        will cancel the entire send mail process

********************************************
***/
SetPointer(HourGlass!)

Do
        lb_noerrors = True
        li_nrecipients = UpperBound( mMsg.Recipient )
        For li_index = 1 To li_nrecipients
```

```
mRet=mSes.mailResolveRecipient(mMsg.Recipient[li_in
dex].Name)
If mRet <> mailReturnSuccess! Then lb_noerrors = False
ls_ret  =  f_mail_error_to_string  (  mRet,  'Resolve
Recipient:', FALSE )
                st_status_bar.text = ' Resolve Recipient
(' + mMsg.Recipient[li_index].Name + '): ' + ls_ret
        Next
        If Not lb_noerrors Then
                Messagebox("Microsoft     Mail","Error
Resolving Name(s)~n~r"+&
                "The   name(s)   not   underlined   are
unresolvable.~n~n~rPlease Correct or Cancel"&
                ,Exclamation!)
                mRet = mSes.mailAddress(mMsg)
                If mRet = mailReturnUserAbort! Then
                st_status_bar.text = "User Canceled Send Mail"
                wf_logoff_mail(mSes, ls_attach_name)
                        Return
                End If
        End If
Loop Until lb_noerrors

/*********************************************
****

        Now,  send  the  mail  message,  including  the
attachment

*********************************************
****/
If UpperBound ( mMsg.Recipient ) < 1 Then
        messagebox ("Powerbuilder send","Mail  must
included at least 1 recipient",Exclamation!)
        wf_logoff_mail(mSes, ls_attach_name)
        return
End If
mRet = mSes.mailsend ( mMsg )
```

```
ls_ret = f_mail_error_to_string ( mRet, 'send Mail:',
FALSE )
st_status_bar.text = ' send Mail: ' + ls_ret

wf_logoff_mail(mSes, ls_attach_name)

//new smtp function
Integer li_rc
SMTPClient lnv_SmtpClient

lnv_SmtpClient = CREATE SMTPClient

//Sets the email-sender information
lnv_SmtpClient.Host = "smtp.testmail.com"
lnv_SmtpClient.Port = 25
lnv_SmtpClient.Username = "tester001@testmail.com"
lnv_SmtpClient.password = "Mypassword001"
lnv_SmtpClient.EnableTLS = False

//Sets the email message
lnv_SmtpClient.Message.SetSender("tester001@testma
il.com","Tester001")
lnv_SmtpClient.Message.AddRecipient("tester002@test
mail.com")
lnv_SmtpClient.Message.Subject    =  "SMTPClient  Test
Message"
lnv_SmtpClient.Message.TextBody    =    "SMTPClient
example message body"

//Sends the email
li_rc = lnv_SmtpClient.Send()

IF li_rc = 1 THEN
        Messagebox('SMTPClient','Mail            sent
successfully')
ELSE
```

```
        Messagebox('SMTPClient'    ,'Email    sending
failed. Return ' + String(li_rc) + '.', StopSign!)
END IF


DESTROY Inv_SmtpClient
//***************send mail button script******
ctr=dw_1.saveas('c:\DataReport.pdf',pdf!,false)
if ctr<0 then
gf_messask("File Not saved-Return code"+string(ctr),1)
end if
openwithparm(w_mail_send,parent.dw_1)
```

Epilogue

There are many commands available in PowerBuilder, which we can check out when required. PowerBuilder has an excellent help feature. One can learn PB by searching for commands from the help. There is also help available online from Appeon Website. And there are online forums where help is available.

For source code and database schemas contact the writer: on these email ids: ravi_kp_com@yahoo.com, ravikiransofttech@gmail.com

This book is a continuation of the book : Develop Software with PowerBuilder, which describes the development of master windows, which was incorporated in the Part 1.

This was done so the readers of this book can develop or practise the software from scratch.

You can get the book on the website: http://ravikirantechonosoft.in   or https://ravikumar.azurewebsites.net

All the links are provided on the above website.

This is a small project compared to others. This application was developed using PowerBuilder with sqlserver2000 on a Windows server. But maintenance was done for 10 years. As requirements and new insurance companies were added, new types of policies came, new processes were introduced by the insurance companies, and constant modifications are necessary. Either in the application or in reports.

Web Application link to download developed using visual studio 2005, combidata.bak for SQL server 2008. These are available in this location in zip format.

https://www.dropbox.com/s/ent1690a1kfxq1g/Web%20Application.zip?dl=0

PowerBuilder Application available at this location: https://www.dropbox.com/s/x17g6in2bgcr987/rk_ghpl_pb11.zip?dl=0

For any other software links to practise contact the writer on the above email.

The best way to practise is to download the book in pdf format from the website and practise on the system.

About the Author

Ravi Kumar Paramkusam is a software professional with over 30 years of experience. He has worked in many industries in multiple languages and domains.